WHAT DO YOU KNOW ABOUT CHIROPRACTIC?

Ralph Lee Smith, author of *The Health Hucksters*, and experienced medical journalist, has been delving into chiropractic for many years. In preparing *At Your Own Risk*, he has traveled from coast to coast:

- —He has been treated as a patient at famous chiropractic clinics.
- —He has visited leading chiropractic schools.
- —He has attended the murder trial of a chiropractor whose eight-year-old patient died of cancer.
- —He was present at a popular "chiropractic research seminar" where the principal subject was how chiropractors could make more money.

READ THE STARTLING FACTS PRESENTED ABOUT CHIROPRACTIC

AT YOUR OWN RISK
is an original Pocket Book edition.

AT YOUR OWN RISK:

The Case against Chiropractic

RALPH LEE SMITH

PUBLISHED BY POCKET BOOKS · NEW YORK

AT YOUR OWN RISK: The Case against Chiropractic

A *Pocket Book* edition published in cooperation with
Parallax Publishing Company, Inc.

1st printing............July, 1969
3rd printing......November, 1970

This original *Pocket Book* edition is printed from
brand-new plates made from newly set, clear, easy-to-read type.
Pocket Book editions are published by Pocket Books, a division of
Simon & Schuster, Inc., 630 Fifth Avenue, New York, N.Y. 10020.
Trademarks registered in the United States and other countries.

L

CONTENTS

The Death of Linda Epping

LINDA EPPING, AN ACTIVE AND EXCEPTIONALLY BEAUTIFUL child, was born February 8, 1953. In the summer of 1961 she developed a slight swelling above her left eye, and her parents took her to the University of California Medical Center in Los Angeles. On July 10th an ophthalmologist (eye specialist) on the staff of the medical school examined her and photographed the growth. Linda was admitted to the hospital the following week.

A biopsy of Linda's tumor taken July 17th showed her to have a particularly dangerous and fast-growing type of cancer whose scientific name is embryonal rhabdomyosarcoma. The tragic news was that immediate surgery was imperative, and that Linda's left eye and the surrounding soft tissue in the orbit would have to be removed. The procedure, the doctors told the Eppings, would at least prolong Linda's life and might possibly save it. The hopeful part of the picture was that, according to the hospital's tests, the cancer was still localized. It had not spread to her brain or to any other part of her body, and apart from the tumor itself Linda was in good health.

Only parents faced with childhood cancer can know

what the Eppings went through in the next four days. At
noon on July 21st Mr. Epping called the physcian and
gave his consent to surgery.

On that same afternoon, when the Eppings were at the
hospital visiting Linda, they fell into conversation with a
couple who told them that a chiropractor named Dr.
Marvin Phillips had cured their son of a brain tumor without an operation.

At the subsequent trial, Mrs. Epping testified that she
called Dr. Phillips, told him of Linda's condition, of the
diagnosis, of the surgery that was to be performed, and
asked if Dr. Phillips could help.

"Yes," Mrs. Epping testified that Dr. Phillips replied,
"absolutely!"

According to Mrs. Epping's testimony, Dr. Phillips repeated his unqualified statement that he could cure
Linda's cancer, both in the phone conversation and later
in his office. She said that Dr. Phillips also described
UCLA hospital as an experimental place where the doctors would use Linda as a guinea pig, cut her up, and kill
her. She testified that he told them to get Linda out of the
hospital and bring her to him the following day.

Mrs. Epping further stated that, when he was asked
how much it would cost, Dr. Phillips said that the fee
would be five hundred dollars, to be paid in advance, and
that there would also be a charge of two hundred to three
hundred dollars a month for medicines.

At 6 o'clock that evening the Eppings, acting against
the advice of the physicians on the case, took Linda out
of the hospital, and the next day they brought her to Dr.
Phillips for treatment.

At the trial Dr. Phillips admitted that he had charged
a $500 fee and that he had also sold medicines to the
Eppings, on which he made a 100% profit. He denied,
however, that he had urged the Eppings to take Linda
out of UCLA Hospital; on the contrary, he said, he had
urged them to keep her in the hospital and to listen to
the doctors there. After they took Linda out of the
hospital, he testified that he told them they should

take her back. He asserted that he had never told them that he could treat cancer, and that, when Linda was under his care, he was not treating her for cancer. Speaking of what chiropractors can do, he said, "we don't cure cancer."[*]

From July 22 until August 13, Linda Epping was treated for her cancer by Dr. Phillips. A fundamental element of the treatment was a daily manipulation of Linda's spine. Dr. Phillips explained that it was a "chiropractic adjustment."

In addition to the adjustments, Dr. Phillips also provided the Eppings with a large supply of vitamins, minerals, food supplements, and laxatives for Linda to take. At the height of the regimen she was required to swallow 124 pills a day, including such items as desiccated ox bile and extract of beef eyes.

While Linda got her daily adjustments and took her pills, the tumor grew swiftly. By August 13th it was the size of a tennis ball and had pushed the eye out of the socket and down along the nose. On this date the Eppings fired Dr. Phillips and called a medical doctor. He urged them to take Linda back to the hospital, but told them frankly that in his opinion the case was now beyond treatment or cure. Nearly beside themselves with grief, the Eppings turned to the courts.

On the late afternoon of December 20, 1961, Los Angeles County Deputy District Attorney John W. Miner was led by Mr. Epping to his daughter's bedside. "Seasoned as I am by observation of many score of autopsies of burned, raped, drowned, strangled, stabbed, shot, accident-mangled, even tumor-ridden bodies," he says, "it was all I could do to keep from abruptly leaving the room. The right half of Linda's face was that of an angel. The left half was covered by a growth so monstrous as to seem beyond nature's capacity to be so cruel and grotesque." Later on, at the trial, the judge prohibited John

---

[*] The question of whether chiropractors attempt to treat cancer is one that will be discussed in this book.

Miner from showing Linda's death pictures to the jury; they were so terrible, he believed, that they might deprive the jury of the ability to weigh the issues rationally.

On December 29, 1961, six weeks before her ninth birthday, Linda Epping died. Miner sought and secured from the grand jury an indictment against Phillips, charging him with second-degree murder, for stating that he could cure Linda and thereby keeping her from medical treatment that doctors stated would have prolonged her life and might have saved it. Phillips was convicted in 1963, but the conviction was set aside by appellate courts. He was retried and reconvicted in December, 1967. His conviction was subsequently upheld on appeal. (See page xi.)

The case—according to Miner, apparently the first one in the seven-hundred-year history of Anglo-American law in which a man was found guilty of murdering with words alone—is a fascinating one for legal scholars. But much more is involved. Chiropractors are taught that chiropractic "adjustment" of the spine *is the true, proper, and correct treatment for many or most types of human disease*. The questions raised by this belief go far beyond the death of a single child. They are cardinal issues of public safety and public health.

My experience has been that most people, including those who have been under chiropractic care, do not know what a D.C.—doctor of chiropractic—is. People I have talked to usually have the vague notion that a chiropractor is a spinal specialist whose training differs from, but is not scientifically inferior to, that of other medical specialties.

The purpose of this book is to set forth what a chiropractor is, what he believes, and what he does. To do so, we must first go back to the nineteenth century and look in on the life and ideas of a grocer and fishmonger of Davenport, Iowa, named Daniel David Palmer. Palmer believed that the golden secret of the ages—the cause and cure of human illness—had been vouchsafed to him and him alone.

The following news story appeared as this book was going to press:

Chiropractor Gets Prison After Murder Appeals Fail

LOS ANGELES, July 9 (UPI)—A chiropractor, Marvin M. Phillips, was sentenced to five years to life in prison today after losing appeals on a second-degree murder conviction in the death of an 8-year-old girl in 1961.

He was convicted twice of second-degree murder in the death of Linda Epping, who succumbed to cancer of the eye in 1961.

Phillips, who continued to practice for eight years after his first conviction, was accused of having the young girl removed from the U.C.L.A. Medical Center after assuring her parents he could cure the girl without surgery for $500.

His first conviction was overturned by an appeal court because of a judicial error.

CHAPTER ONE

The Iowa Grocer's Dream

DANIEL DAVID PALMER, THE INVENTOR OF CHIROPRACTIC (the term is used both as an adjective and a noun), was born near Toronto, Ontario, Canada, on March 7, 1845. He was one of six children of Thomas Palmer, a shoemaker, and his wife Katherine. In April, 1865, when he was twenty, he and his twenty-two-year-old brother Thomas left home together and headed for the United States. After walking for thirty days they reached Buffalo, where they spent their last savings for boat passage to Detroit. There, according to Daniel, they slept on grain sacks near a boat pier, ate a persimmon for breakfast, and found temporary work.

Thomas's wanderings brought him to the town of Medford in Oklahoma Territory, where he eventually entered the real estate business and lived to a ripe old age. By the 1880's Daniel had married and settled in What Cheer, Iowa, where he made a living as a grocer and fish peddler. He was to marry five more times before his life ended in lonely bitterness in California in 1913.

1

Improbably enough, beneath the exterior of this man there burned the narrow, fierce heart of a prophet. He searched for revelations and, when he found them, tolerated no doubts even among his closest followers and his family. If he had been born in Arabia he might have risen from obscurity to lead a Holy War. As it was, he was destined to found a new sect of true believers.

The nineteenth century was a great age for medical and psychic cults, and Palmer was engrossed in them. He looked into osteopathy, then in its rough-and-ready infancy. He dabbled in phrenology and spiritualism. In 1886, apparently feeling some kind of "call," he moved from What Cheer to Davenport, Iowa, and set up a "magnetic healing" studio in that city's tenderloin district. Practitioners of magnetic healing believed that they belonged to a unique group of human beings whose personal magnetism was so great that it gave them the power to cure disease. The truth was much more mundane: the untutored healers had developed a crude knowledge of hypnotism.

For nine years Palmer immersed himself in the practice of personal magnetism, providing no family life for his three daughters or for his son Bartlett Joshua. During this time Palmer was involved in a search that had come to be the passion of his life. He was looking for nature's Great Secret—the cause of human disease. Not *causes*. In medieval fashion, he believed in a single cause, a single factor responsible for all illnesses. With that single cause discovered, a single method for eliminating it could be found, and the curse of disease would pass from the human race.

"One question was always uppermost in my mind in my search for the cause of disease," he said. "I desired to know why one person was ailing and his associate, eating at the same table, working in the same shop, at the same bench, was not. *Why?* What difference was there in the two persons that caused one to have pneumonia, catarrh, typhoid, or rheumatism, while his partner, similarly situated, escaped? *Why?"*

Palmer struggled with his demon, and at last it yielded up its secret. "This question [as to the cause of disease] had worried thousands for centuries," he said, "and was answered in September, 1895." Actually, his account of his discovery is in some ways so bizarre that one cannot be sure how much of it really happened and how much of it was supplied by the workings of a feverish brain. For whatever it is worth, here is Palmer's story.

On the block where his offices were located, Palmer says, there worked a janitor named Harvey Lillard who had been deaf for seventeen years. Palmer made inquiry and found that "when he [Lillard] was exerting himself in a cramped, stooping position, he felt something give way in his back and immediately became deaf."

Palmer examined Lillard and found a subluxated (misaligned) vertebra in his spine. "I reasoned that if that vertebra was replaced," said Palmer, "the man's hearing should be restored. With this object in view, a half-hour's talk persuaded Mr. Lillard to allow me to replace it."

Palmer laid Lillard down on his stomach on an examining couch, and applied a firm pressure to the vertebra with his hands. The vertebra moved back into place, "and soon the man could hear as before."

Magnetic healer Palmer could hardly be expected to know that the nerves of hearing are self-contained in the head and do not reach the spine. And the reader is entitled to wonder how Palmer discussed Lillard's problem with him for a half hour while Lillard was deaf. But Palmer believed that he was on the track of the Great Secret.

"Shortly after this relief from deafness, I had a case of heart trouble which was not improving. I examined the spine and found a displaced vertebra pressing against the

---

* D. D. Palmer, *Text-Book of the Science, Art and Philosophy of Chiropractic, Founded on Tone* (Portland, Ore.: Portland Printing House Company, 1910, republished 1966), p. 18.

nerves which innervate the heart. I adjusted the vertebra and gave immediate relief. . . ."

"Then I began to reason," he continued, "if two diseases, so dissimilar as deafness and heart trouble, came from impingement, a pressure on nerves, were not other disease [*sic*] due to a similar cause?"*

To Palmer, the truth was clear: "A subluxated vertebra, a verterbral bone, is the cause of 95 percent of all diseases."** "Luxated bones," he explains, press against nerves.

> By their displacement and pressure they elongate the pathway of the nerve in a manner similar to that by which an impingement upon a wire of a musical instrument induces it to become taut by displacing it from a direct line. This pressure upon a nerve creates greater tension, increased vibration, and consequently an increased amount of heat. Heat alters tissue; altered tissue modifies the transmission of impulses; modified impulses cause functions to be performed abnormally.†

So there it was—the secret of disease revealed. Disease is caused by nerves that are pinched by misaligned spinal vertebrae. The cure consists in exerting a manual pressure on the misaligned vertebrae and forcing them back into place. Daniel David Palmer believed it in 1895, and, as we shall see, it remains the basic concept of chiropractic today.

Palmer confided his discovery to a friend, Reverend Samuel Weed. Weed suggested that the new marvel be called "chiropractic," from the Greek *cheiro* and *praktikos*, "done by hand."

---

* *Ibid.*, pp. 18, 19.

** "The other five percent," he said, "is caused by displaced bones, other than those of the vertebral column, more especially those of the tarsus, metatarsus and phalanges, which, by their displacement, are the cause of bunions and corns" (*Ibid.*, p. 56).

† *Ibid.*, p. 58.

4

At first Palmer did not want to let the world in on his awe-inspiring secret. He even took down a mirror on his office wall when it occurred to him that his patients might be using it to watch what he was doing. But before the end of 1895 his attitude had changed, and instead of concealing his discovery, he had set up the Palmer School of Chiropractic to teach it. The course ran for three months; the student learned how to adjust spines, and got a quick medical education from *Dr. Pierce's Family Medical Adviser*. The Palmer School began with a tuition of $500, dropped it to $300, then raised it to $450 with a $50 discount for cash. The only admission requirement was the ability to pay the fee.

Of his early students and disciples, by far the most important from the standpoint of the future of chiropractic was his own son Bartlett Joshua, usually known simply by his initials B. J. Like many discoverers and prophets, Daniel David Palmer was almost entirely deficient in the worldly arts of commercial success. His son was a commercial and public relations genius. The result was that Daniel David died penniless while B. J., who took over the Palmer School and the leadership of chiropractic, died a multimillionaire.

While his father was occupied in discovering the cause and cure of human illness, B. J., who was born in 1881, apparently experienced a grim childhood. In 1949 he published a book entitled *The Bigness of the Fellow Within,* (Davenport: Chiropractic Fountain Head, 1949) the preface to which was written by Herbert C. Hender, dean of the Palmer School. Speaking of B. J., Hender said:

> The first twenty years of this boy's life were spent in being educated to hate people and everything they did or were connected with.
>
> His mother died when he was one-and-a-half years old. From then on, he was at the mercy of five cruel stepmothers, each worse than the one before.
>
> Because of brutality at home, he was often forced

5

to sleep in dry-goods boxes in alleys, often with the weather below zero, curled like a rat in a nest with paper packing, with open face of box backed up against brick walls; under kitchen sinks of hotels; or by boilers of boats on the Mississippi.

He worked for a time as floor scrubber, window washer, spittoon cleaner, and special-delivery boy for a department store in his home town, getting three dollars per week as salary. He used to take out five cents a week for a bag of peanuts. This was his only luxury, for which he regularly got a beating. . . .

This is just a beginning of tales he could tell of horrors of his early family and home life.*

Like his father, B. J. had little schooling. He was questioned about it when he testified in a Wisconsin trial involving a chiropractor in 1910:**

Q. How old are you?

A. I was twenty-eight last September.

Q. And you have been studying chiropractics sixteen years?

A. I have.

Q. Then you began the study of chiropractics at the age of twelve?

A. At the age of twelve I was practicing in the field as a practitioner.†

Q. Of what?

A. Chiropractics. At the age of eleven I was kicked from home, forced to make my living.

Q. What education had you up to that time?

A. Common sense.

---

* *The Bigness of the Fellow Within*, p. xv.

** *State of Wisconsin* v. *S. R. Jansheski*. Tried in the District Court of Milwaukee, Wis., December, 1910. Portions of testimony reprinted in *A Chiropractic Catechism* (American Medical Association Bureau of Legal Medicine and Legislation, n.d.), p. 6.

† B. J. is in error here, since he was twelve in 1893–1894, before his father invented chiropractic.

6

Q. What education had you had at the time you began the practice of chiropractics?
A. Common sense.
Q. None other?
A. Well, horse reasoning.
Q. Any other?
A. Good judgment.
Q. Any other, I ask you?
A. That is enough.*

The beginnings of B. J.'s association with his father in launching chiropractic are obscure. "When in his teens," says Hender, "he [B. J.] was forced by circumstances beyond his control to begin his professional career as a Chiropractor, starting in his own home town where he once lived as an alley-cat and wharf-rat."* Whatever kind of working relationship they may have established, it is clear that father and son were both involved in operating the school almost from the outset. By 1902 B. J. had grown a beard to look older than his twenty years and was teaching at the new institution. Soon it was aggressive, precocious B. J., not his father, who was running the school and presiding over the nationwide spread of chiropractic.

Matters came to a head in 1906 when B. J. was twenty-four. Father and son were both charged with practicing medicine without a license. The father was brought to trial first—the reason, says B. J. cryptically, is "best known by local merchants." He was found guilty and went to jail. B. J. was never tried.

After Daniel David was released from jail, B. J. bought out his business. Fcr the Palmer School B. J. paid his father $2,196.79, plus one normal spine, one abnormal spine, six vertebrae, and Daniel David's choice of any twelve books from the school library. Daniel David Palmer left Davenport, deeply embittered. His bitterness increased when, in the same year, B. J. published the

---

* B. J. Palmer, *The Bigness of the Fellow Within*, p. xvii.

world's first book on chiropractic. Daniel claimed that "most of its contents, which gave the principles of the science and somewhat of the art of adjusting vertebrae, were from my pen."

From the time he left Davenport until his death seven years later, Daniel's life was that of a wanderer. He journeyed to Medford, Oklahoma, where his brother had settled, and there went back into the grocery business, but soon abandoned it and left for the Pacific coast. In 1910, in Portland, Oregon, he published an immense, chaotic book entitled *Text-Book of the Science, Art and Philosophy of Chiropractic, Founded on Tone.* The 1,007-page volume is full of unhappy diatribes against other chiropractors and against his son.

In 1911 he returned to Davenport and founded a new chiropractic school, the Universal Chiropractic College, two blocks from the now-thriving Palmer School. Within a year, however, he abandoned this, too, and went to California.

In July, 1913, the Palmer School of Chiropractic held its annual Lyceum and Homecoming, complete with a parade through the streets of the town. B. J. Palmer rode in an automobile in the parade. Suddenly a ghost materialized on the sidewalk—Daniel David Palmer. Waving a small American flag, he insisted on leading the alumni procession, but was prohibited from doing so by the marshal of the parade, who was a student at the school. An altercation ensued. B. J. drove up in his automobile. Words passed between father and son. What happened after that depends on whom you believe. Daniel David claimed that B. J. struck him with his automobile, and D. D.'s friends and allies later produced affidavits of witnesses to prove it. B. J. flatly denied it, and produced many more affidavits to this effect than D. D.'s cohorts were able to muster.

That night Daniel David Palmer left Davenport for the last time. Three months later he died in Los Angeles. He stipulated that his son was not to come to his funeral.

The executors of the father's estate filed a civil damages

suit against B. J., alleging that B. J. had struck Daniel David with his car and that this had contributed to the father's death. After pending in court for several months, the action was dropped without prejudice, and was never reinstated. The Scott County District Attorney also sought a murder indictment against B. J., but two grand juries refused to return a true bill.

Meanwhile B. J. was on his way to making a fortune. Ironically, a by-product of his immense personal success was a tremendous diffusion of the cult. Under B. J. Palmer's long reign, which ended only with his death in 1961, chiropractic achieved such a wide base of practice and activity that it continues to flourish in the Space Age.

"Our school," B. J. said frankly, "is on a business, not a professional basis. We manufacture chiropractors." He advertised widely for students, and to a prospect who was worried about having a spotty educational background he wrote, "In regard to educational qualifications, do not allow this to annoy you. We hold no entrance examinations." An inveterate sloganeer, he decorated the grounds, walls, stair risers, and even the rest rooms of the Palmer School with such sayings as "The world is your cow—but you must do the milking," and "Early to bed and early to rise—work like hell and advertise." A slogan on the wall of the ladies' rest room said, "Beauty is only skin-deep. Many people need peeling."

The course was lengthened to nine months, and a correspondence course leading to a Doctor of Chiropractic degree was made available for those who could not attend in person. Business was soon booming. Chiropractic spread rapidly, the Palmer School became known among chiropractors as "the Fountainhead," and B. J. became the guru of the cult.

Bemused by B. J.'s success, other chiropractors rushed to become educators. It has been estimated that as many as 600 chiropractic schools have existed in the United States, many of them fly-by-night operations, "manufacturing" chiropractors in shabby rooms or lofts, or granting degrees by mail. Many chiropractors in practice today

obtained their doctor's degrees from one of these operations. In 1945 *Medical World News* reported that it was
still possible to obtain a mail-order doctor of chiropractic
degree from a Chicago college for $127.50.

B. J. had no objection to the proliferation of schools.
In addition to running the Palmer School, he conducted a
brisk mail-order business, selling chiropractors throughout
the nation such items as adjustment tables, miniature
spine sections, and portraits of B. J. Palmer. He also
made available to them, on lease only, a gadget called
the Neurocalometer, about which we will hear more
presently.

As the money poured in, B. J. created a miniature Ivy
League campus for the Palmer School complete with bell
tower and chimes. With characteristic perspicacity he
also became a radio pioneer, establishing radio station
WOC (Wonders of Chiropractic) in Davenport and
securing control of WHO in Des Moines. During his life
he also wrote thirty-eight books, including one called
Radio Salesmanship which went through a number of
printings. In his spare time he made himself available for
lectures on business psychology.

A prodigious earner, he was also a prodigious spender.
He purchased several summer residences, including one
in Sarasota, Florida, near his friend and fellow showman,
John Ringling North (among other things, Palmer was a
circus buff). With his family he traveled over a million
miles around the world, and had mountains of relics and
gimcracks shipped back to Davenport from the far corners
of the earth.

The treasures and trash from his voyages overflowed
his house and spilled out over the campus. The garden
of the Palmer School's clinic contains, among other things,
a torii—red wooden entrance gate—from a Japanese
temple, bronze flamingos, cast-iron elks, and an immense
anchor. Another section of the campus, called "A Little
Bit o' Heaven," contains innumerable items including a
ninety-ton Buddha, eight Hindu idols carved from lava,
a marble sculpture called *The Birth of Venus*, Chinese

Foo dogs, satsuma vases, *The Pearly Gates of St. Peter* inlaid with semiprecious stones, a replica of the Black Hole of Calcutta, a bench from King Tut's tomb, and "the world's two largest clamshells." In his own house it is reported that Palmer kept an immense collection of swords and sabers and a large assortment of shrunken heads.

Also on the campus is a large greenhouse, over two stories high, filled with exotic trees and plants. On the outside wall, inlaid in marble and multicolored tile, is a slogan reading, "Anything I do you don't do is queer. Queer, isn't it? B. J."

Once, when Palmer was traveling with his family in Hawaii, he received a cable that his Saint Bernard dog, Big Ben, had had a heart attack and died while chasing a poodle across the street. B. J. promptly cancelled the rest of his trip, booked passage home for the whole family, and had Big Ben stuffed and placed under the piano in the living room.

Throughout his life B. J. affirmed his belief in the pure doctrine of chiropractic as enunciated by his father. "*Chiropractic* principle has the vertebral subluxation as *the cause* of *all* dis-ease," he wrote. "*Chiropractic* practice has the vertebral adjustment as *the cure* of *all* disease." "No man ever questioned his sincerity toward chiropractic," says his son, David Daniel Palmer (the founder's names reversed), in a book published in 1967. However, when I traveled to Davenport to secure information for this chapter, I made some interesting discoveries.

Although B. J. alleged in his public writings that chiropractic treatment would cure all diseases, when he was ill he went to see medical doctors in Davenport. Among other things, these doctors discovered that B. J.'s own spine was about the worst possible advertisement for the value of chiropractic treatment that could be imagined. When B. J. developed a urinary tract problem his spine was X-rayed by a competent group of specialists. "He had the worst-looking spine of anyone you've ever seen,"

11

the doctor who supervised the X rays told me. "It showed very advanced degenerative arthritis with marked curvature." Later he developed cancer of the colon and received medical treatment for it, including surgery. Part of the colon was removed, but it was not possible to check the cancer, and B. J. died of it in 1961 at age seventy-nine. His son, David Daniel, age fifty-five, assumed control of the family affairs.

David Daniel's accession as president of the Palmer School was a watershed. With B. J.'s death the Old Guard passed. B. J.'s loud-checkered vests and Van Dyke beard, with all they symbolized, are now being replaced by the gray flannel suit. But unfortunately, the thrust of the changes has not been to accept science. Instead, the identical doctrine is being decked out in a dress more suitable to our times.

The Palmer School is now the Palmer College of Chiropractic. "We threw out the flamboyancy, the things that kept it from being a college," David Daniel Palmer says. "We gave it a new image; academic standards; a college spirit."

Some of the slogans have been removed from the college's buildings and walls—and, more interestingly, B. J.'s books are not on the college library's shelves. It would apparently now require considerable industry on the part of a Palmer student to learn some of the information about the origin and growth of chiropractic that uninhibited B. J. put into such volumes as *The Bigness of the Fellow Within*. When I looked up B. J. Palmer in the library's card index, a card said, "The works of B. J. Palmer are not cataloged. Inquire at desk." When I asked at the desk, the librarian on duty said, "We don't have very many of them. They are locked up and can't be checked out."

Twenty-two states now require chiropractors to have one or two years' college credit, in addition to their chiropractic educations, in order to be licensed. David Daniel Palmer founded and is president of Palmer Junior College, which shares facilities with the Palmer College of Chiropractic. The junior college is accredited and grants two-year associate of arts degrees. If one wishes, one can graduate from the junior college and then go on to the chiropractic course.

The family-owned Palmer Broadcasting Company has extensive radio and TV holdings, the value of which was estimated in 1965 at $15 to $20 million.

In 1967, Iowa Governor Harold Hughes nominated Palmer to fill a vacancy on the nine-member Board of Regents, which supervises the state's institutions of higher education, including the University of Iowa College of Medicine. There was a furor when the Iowa Medical Society objected. The Iowa Senate voted 35 to 24 to confirm the nomination, but this was six votes short of the required two-thirds majority. His name remained before the Senate on a motion to reconsider while his backers tried to rally enough votes. But the governor then withdrew the nomination on Palmer's request. Palmer wrote the governor that the "controversy engendered by a minority group with vested interests has subjected you, personally, to much embarrassment."

David Daniel Palmer and his family live in a twenty-room brick house surrounded by evergreens, overlooking the Mississippi River, on whose dark wharves B. J. slept as a child seventy-five years ago. In the face of all the available evidence of twentieth-century medical science, David Daniel and the nation's other chiropractors continue to base much or all of their approach to human disease on the Iowa grocer's dream.

Near the center of the Palmer campus are two large granite shafts, one surmounted by an immense bust of Daniel David Palmer and the other by an equally large bust of B. J. In a niche in each shaft, protected by a panel of glass, are bronze urns containing their ashes. The prophet and his son are at peace.

CHAPTER TWO

Chiropractic Today

> Q. What are the principal functions of the spine?
> A. To support the head
> To support the ribs
> To support the chiropractor.
> —B. J. Palmer, *Answers* (1952)

ACCORDING TO THE INTERNATIONAL CHIROPRACTORS Association, over 30 million Americans have received chiropractic care. Today, instead of fading away in the face of modern science, chiropractic is experiencing a renaissance.

In states that permit it, some chiropractors are aggressively advertising in newspapers for patients, using case histories and testimonials to prove that chiropractic helps and cures numerous diseases.

After holding out for years, the legislatures of two of the nation's most populous states, Massachusetts and New York, succumbed to the ceaseless pressures of the chiropractic lobby in the 1960's and passed laws licensing chiropractors.

Two paperback books extolling chiropractic—*Your Health and Chiropractic* by Thorp McClusky (New York: Pyramid Books, 1962) and *Chiropractic: A Modern Way to Health* by Dr. Julius Dintenfass, D.C. (New York: Pyramid Books, 1966)—have been published and are available at bookstores, drugstores, and airports. The latter book was offered for sale in a display ad in the cosmopolitan New York newspaper *The Village Voice* in April, 1968, which reaches the nation's cultural and professional elite.*

In Fort Worth, Texas, the Parker Chiropractic Research Foundation pours out reams of literature for chiropractors to disseminate among their patients and in their communities, and conducts three-day seminars for chiropractors on how to increase their incomes (see Chapter Four). Other chiropractic groups are turning out attractive new booklets and leaflets emphasizing the theme that chiropractic is a modern, scientific branch of the healing arts.

In a major new departure, certain chiropractors have recently been moving into the field of mental and emotional health, alleging that spinal adjustments are beneficial to sufferers of conditions ranging from neurosis to schizophrenia (see Chapter Seven).

All this activity has been paying off. The American spine is probably supporting the chiropractor more handsomely now than at any time in the past.

It is not certain how many active chiropractors there are in the United States. The 1960 census listed 14,360 persons who gave their occupation as chiropractor. A publication of the American Chiropractic Association, however, claims that there are 25,000, and a public relations firm for chiropractors gives the figure as 35,000. The discrepancies may be partly accounted for by the

---

* For a discussion of one of the testimonials that appears in these books, see Chapter Ten.

fact that many chiropractors do not practice full time, and may have cited some other activity as their principal occupation when interviewed by the census-taker.

The 1967 *Directory* issued by the Council of State Chiropractic Examining Boards states that, as of January 1, 1966, there were 23,634 currently active chiropractic licenses in the United States and 772 in Canada, making a combined North American total of 24,406.* Of these, 173 of the United States licenses and 6 of the Canadian were licenses granted by reciprocity in 1966, and an additional number of the total undoubtedly represents chiropractors holding more than one state license. A figure of 20,000 would probably be a fair estimate of the number of persons holding one or more active licenses to practice chiropractic.**

How big is the chiropractic profession economically? This author's guess is that chiropractors treat about 3 million people a year, and that the profession's annual income is about $300 million.

Figures in the *Textbook of Office Procedure and Practice Building for the Chiropractic Profession,†* published by the Parker Chiropractic Research Foundation, indicate that the initial physical exam and X ray given by a chiropractor is likely to cost the patient about $40. The chiropractor is then likely to recommend a series of twenty to fifty adjustments, which will cost the patient about $4 each. Some patients, of course, will abandon treatment before the full course of adjustments is completed.

The number of patients treated annually by licensed chiropractors varies widely. At one end of the scale are

---

* Of these, 537 were new licenses issued in 1966, indicating the continuing influx of new blood into the profession.

** Chiropractors are licensed on the basis of examinations given by state licensing boards. Requirements are established by legislation, and differ in each state. Further information on chiropractic licensure appears in Chapters Six and Twelve.

† Fort Worth, N.D.

chiropractors who make their principal living at some other occupation and may see only a few patients a year. At the other end are chiropractors with highly active practices who operate private clinics and treat between 500 and 1,000 persons a year.

If we estimate that the average licensed chiropractor sees 150 patients a year, then 3 million people annually receive the benefits of the gospel according to Palmer. If the chiropractor receives an average of $100 from each patient, then chiropractic is a $300-million business.

Of course, it is clear that many chiropractors make far more than the $15,000-a-year income that would be the average if we accept the foregoing as working figures. At the Parker Seminar on Practice Building which I attended in 1967, I was told that a number of those attending had incomes in the $100,000-a-year range. Several others assured me that few of the chiropractors who attend the seminars regularly have incomes as low as $15,000.

One of the early converts to chiropractic was an Oklahoma City lawyer named Willard Carver, who established a chiropractic school in that city a few years after the Palmer School was launched in Davenport. Carver and Palmer diverged on ideology. Carver developed the view that chiropractic should employ, in addition to the chiropractic adjustment, various other types and methods of treatment such as physical and nutritional therapy, and, in some instances, methods rejected by conventional medicine. Palmer disagreed. Only chiropractic adjustments, he said, dealt with and eliminated the cause of disease. Other types of treatment, therefore, could have no higher value than the elimination of symptoms.

This schism among the faithful has never been healed. Today chiropractors who stick to adjustments as the almost exclusive treatment for illness are called "straights." Those who supplement adjustments with other means of treatment are called "mixers." The Carver School (no longer in existence) was for a long time the chief disseminator of the mixer philosophy. The Palmer School was, and still is, the headquarters of the straight approach. The bitterness of the dispute has been deepened because, like medieval controversies over the characteristics of angels, it cannot be resolved by recourse to science. The two groups even have their own associations—the International Chiropractors Association for the straights, the American Chiropractic Association for the mixers. Chiropractic schools align themselves with one or the other of the groups and are recognized only by the association for that group.

In 1967 the two associations entered into correspondence to try to resolve their differences. But, as always in the past, they failed, and the effort ended in mutual recriminations. "Evidently we overlooked the influence of political, power-hungry individuals associated with chiropractic whose apparent ambition is to keep the profession divided," L. W. Rutherford, D.C., president of the International Chiropractors Association, wrote to Sidney C. Birdsley, D.C., president of the American Chiropractic Association. "Is it going to take a major catastrophe in chiropractic to make ACA see the need of chiropractic unity and one organization representing this profession?"

Dr. Birdsley gave back as good as he got. ". . . until the ICA recognizes the facts of life and demonstrates a truly sincere desire for unity, rather than an inclination towards making overtures for propaganda purposes only," he replied, "the ACA will have to go it alone."

On the cause of disease, the International Chiropractors Association (the "straights") says:

The philosophy of chiropractic is based upon the premise that disease or abnormal function is caused by interference with nerve transmission and expression, due to pressure, strain, or tension upon the spinal nerves, as a result of bony segments of the

19

vertebral column deviating from their normal juxta-position.

On the treatment of disease it says:

The practice of chiropractic consists of analysis of any interference with normal nerve transmission and expression, and the correction thereof by an adjustment with the hands of the abnormal deviations of the bony articulations of the vertebral column for the restoration and maintenance of health without the use of drugs or surgery.[*]

The American Chiropractic Association (the "mixers") says:

Chiropractic practice is the specific adjustment and manipulation of the articulations and adjacent tissues of the body, particularly of the spinal column, for the correction of nerve interference and includes the use of recognized diagnostic methods, as indicated. Patient care is conducted with due regard for environmental, nutritional, and psychotherapeutic factors, as well as first aid, hygiene, sanitation, rehabilitation and related procedures designed to restore or maintain normal nerve function.[**]

To what extent do today's chiropractors believe in the gospel according to Daniel David Palmer and in its modern versions given above? This question was one of many that were considered by a Department of Health, Education and Welfare study group. When the 90th Congress passed the Medicare Act in 1967 (Public Law 90-248, Social Security Amendments), it asked the Secretary of HEW to study the question of whether certain types of practitioners, who are not medical doctors, should be in-

---

[*] *International Chiropractors Review,* International Chiropractors Association (March, 1964), p. 2.

[**] American Chiropractic Association *Journal* (November, 1963), p. 13.

cluded in the program. Chiropractors and naturopaths* were among the types of practitioners whose status was to be studied.

HEW named an eight-man expert review panel to serve as technical and scientific advisers for the study of chiropractic and naturopathy. The members of the panel were selected, HEW said, "on the basis of their scientific background and high professional reputations in their respective fields." Professional associations representing chiropractors and naturopaths were invited to make presentations and submit material, which were reviewed along with material and information compiled by HEW.

HEW's Report, entitled *Independent Practitioners Under Medicare,* was transmitted to Congress by HEW Secretary Wilbur J. Cohen on December 28, 1968. It recommended against the inclusion of both chiropractors and naturopaths in the Medicare program.** On the specific question of whether all chiropractors believe in the chiropractic theory of disease, the Report says, "It should be pointed out here that many chiropractors do not believe that a subluxation is the only cause of disease, that spinal analysis is the only diagnostic tool, or that the chiropractic adjustment is the only valid treatment." However, says the Report, "because the chiropractic approach to treatment is so greatly influenced by its philosophy, the main

---

* "Naturopathy" is the treatment of illness by "properly arranging the intake of foods first, to eliminate the toxins in the body, and second, to build normal cells, blood, tissues and secretions" ("The Philosophy of Naturopathy," undated leaflet, no publisher given, copy in author's file). In addition to diet it emphasizes the achieving of "a proper mental attitude" which "attracts a health atmosphere," and eschews the use of drugs for healing or preventing disease. (The author of this book got a doctor of naturopathy degree by mail for $12 from a diploma mill in 1967 without doing any work.)

** The composition of HEW's expert review panel, and the complete text of the Report's conclusions and recommendations on chiropractic, appear in Appendix A. *Independent Practitioners Under Medicare* is hereinafter referred to as the HEW Report.

therapeutic concern is to correct the subluxation . . . the concepts of the subluxation and of the spinal analysis and adjustment form the basis of chiropractic thinking and activities; they are greatly emphasized over other concepts of diagnosis and treatment and disease causation."[*]

What illnesses do chiropractors treat? "Since the philosophy of chiropractic is all-encompassing," says the HEW Report, "its practitioners treat nearly every type of illness."[**] This is amply confirmed by a review of chiropractic literature.

A chart in the Parker Chiropractic Research Foundation's *Textbook of Office Procedure and Practice Building for the Chiropractic Profession,* pages 151–52, shows the average number of adjustments given by chiropractors for various disorders.[†] The chart, says the Foundation, is based on reports of approximately 250,000 cases, and lists ninety-two maladies. Here are some of the conditions and the average number of adjustments given by chiropractors to treat them:

CONDITION	AVERAGE NUMBER OF ADJUSTMENTS
Acne	28.2
Angina pectoris	32.1
Appendicitis	22.3
Arthritis	49.0
Deafness	33.2[†]
Diabetes	51.3
Epilepsy	76.1
Eye disorders	42.5
Goiter	43.3
Heart disorders	36.8

---

[*] HEW Report, pp. 165–66.

[**] *Op. cit.,* p. 157.

[†] Chiropractors seem to have lost their touch since the days of D. D. Palmer, who cured Harvey Lillard's deafness with a single adjustment.

Hemorrhoids	50.9
High blood pressure	32.1
Jaundice	84.1
Kidney disorders	43.2
Menstrual disorders	33.1
Nephritis	34.1
Obesity	47.3
Palsy	63.7
Parkinson's disease	57.6
Pneumonia	28.6
Polio (acute)	34.6
Polio (chronic)	51.3
Prostate trouble	42.9
Rheumatic fever	52.2
Ulcers	46.2

Cancer does not appear on this chart.* At the Phillips trial, the dean of the Los Angeles College of Chiropractic, Phillips' alma mater, testified that students there were not taught a specific cure for cancer, and were told that it could not be cured by manipulation, vitamins, or food supplements. There is, however, nothing in chiropractic

---

* The *Parker Textbook*'s handling of the cancer question is fascinating. If a patient asks about it over the phone, the book suggests that the chiropractor should *not* indicate that treatment of cancer is beyond the scope of his activities. Here is the question-and-answer as given in the book:

"Q: 'What can chiropractic do for such diseases as cancer?' (Any other uncommon or questionable disease.)

"A: 'In the thirty years I have been in practice, I have seen very many serious conditions and helped a great number of them. Chiropractic therapy has grown from one man in one town to twenty thousand men all over the world, and one of the reasons has been the almost miraculous results in many seemingly impossible cases. I am sure you understand, Mrs. Jones, it would be necessary for me to see and examine you before your question can be answered fully. I can give you an appointment at 10:00 A.M. or 2:00 P.M. Which time would be more convenient?'" (*Ibid.*, pp. 65, 67.)

theory that excludes cancer from the diseases supposedly caused by subluxations, and there is no doubt that some chiropractors have treated it. Others, lacking diagnostic skills, may treat cancer victims without knowing of the presence of the malignancies.

In a survey made in 1963 for the American Chiropractic Association, 7 percent of the chiropractors surveyed said that they treated cancer and 8 percent said that they treated leukemia.* Until a state law prohibited chiropractors in Colorado from treating cancer, the Spears Chiropractic Hospital in Denver advertised its cancer treatments throughout the nation (see Chapter Seven). A booklet that I purchased at the Palmer College of Chiropractic bookstore in 1968** sets forth "case records to demonstrate the effectiveness of chiropractic with cases medically diagnosed as multiple sclerosis, encephalitis or sleeping sickness, epilepsy, sciatica, cirrhosis and cancer of the liver, and tumors."

The words "medically dignosed" in this statement have a significance that the reader might not at first catch. Although some chiropractic groups have reported with alacrity the illnesses that supposedly respond to chiropractic treatment, a good deal of chiropractic literature, and many individual chiropractors, maintain that actual diagnosis of illnesses is unimportant for a chiropractor. If one is curious enough to ask how, under these circumstances, the chiropractors know that their patients were suffering from the diseases listed in the charts, one is usually told that the patients first went to an M.D., who diagnosed them, and then went to a chiropractor to get their conditions treated.

The lack of interest of some chiropractors in knowing what maladies their patients have stems from the chiropractic theory itself. Medical science knows that different

---

* HEW Report, pp. 157–58.

** "Neurocalometer–Neurocalograph–Neurotempometer Research as Applied to Eight B. J. Palmer Chiropractic Clinic Cases." (No place or date of publication is indicated.)

diseases have different causes and require different treatments. Correct diagnosis is therefore central to successful therapy. By contrast, chiropractic theory states that most or all illnesses come from a single source. The chiropractor may therefore believe that his task is not to identify the affliction but to roll the patient over and adjust the spinal subluxations that he rarely fails to discover. The illness, according to the theory, is likely to disappear, whatever it was, so why diagnose it?

"Because of emphasis constantly being placed upon diagnosis by the medical profession," says the booklet that I purchased in the Palmer College of Chiropractic bookstore, "it is difficult for the average lay person to realize that the chiropractor need not diagnose and therefore diagnosis is unimportant to him."

B. J. Palmer of course agrees. "The Chiropractor pays little, if any, attention to symptoms or pathologies. Patient can come to the B. J. Palmer Chiropractic Clinic, Davenport, Iowa, and be deaf, dumb, and blind—not telling or indicating anything—and we could and would locate THE CAUSE [in the spine] of whatever, wherever he had: adjust him, and send him home well."*

B. J.'s grammar might not be perfect, but his meaning is plain. It raises fascinating questions. Suppose a patient went to a chiropractor with symptoms that would clearly indicate the possible presence of a dangerous illness. Would the chiropractor recognize the symptoms? Would he try to find out if the patient actually had that illness? Or would he simply adjust the patient's back?

Again, suppose a patient had a spine with no detectable medical abnormality. Would the chiropractor nevertheless discover that it was subluxated in such a way as to cause disease? If the patient went to two chiropractors, would they both discover subluxations? Would they find them in the same place?

Some experiences relating to these questions are described in the next chapter.

---

* *Bigness of the Fellow Within*, p. 56.

Who goes to chiropractors? The answer seems to be—everybody. Chiropractic patients come from every strata of our society and from every walk of life.

John D. Rockefeller, Sr., was a chiropractic patient Thorp McClusky says in his book *Your Health and Chiropractic*. Among other chiropractic patients, according to McClusky, have been Presidents Coolidge and Eisenhower, and such notables as Fred Allen, Clara Bow, Eddie Cantor, Enrico Caruso, Clarence Darrow, Mahatma Gandhi, Elbert Hubbard, and Mme. Chiang Kai-shek."[*]

From his own knowledge the author can add the name of the late Senator William Langer, former chairman of the Senate Foreign Relations Committee. If an item appearing in a recent issue of a chiropractic publication is correct, former President Harry S. Truman must be added to the list of United States Presidents who have had their subluxations adjusted.

Actually, my experience has been that nearly everyone has either been to a chiropractor, or has a family member or a friend who has been to a chiropractor. Among my own friends, chiropractic patients include a high school teacher, an assistant film producer, and one of the most successful lawyers on the West Coast.

Chiropractors also treat many people from poor and less well-educated segments of the population. Here, as elsewhere, chiropractors are conducting an intensive publicity drive to secure whole legions of new patients.

No matter what aspect of chiropractic one considers, there is no doubt that it is a major factor in American health care, and that it is aggressively seeking an even larger role. For that reason, one cannot be indifferent to the unanimous voice of science, which states that chiropractic theory has about the same medical validity as voodoo or witchcraft.

---

[*] P. 20.

CHAPTER THREE

I Get the Treatment

"Oof!"

I was kneeling with my head on a little headrest that reminded me of a chopping block. The student chiropractor in the Palmer College of Chiropractic Clinic, a young blond Hercules, stood over me with his hands planted, one over the other, firmly at a midpoint in my unsupported back. Suddenly he pushed down with all his strength and weight. "There must be a better way to get this information," I thought to myself as Hercules moved his hands a little farther down my spine. But I didn't say it out loud. Instead, I said "Ouch!" as he did it again.

Actually, although I was left with a sore back for a couple of weeks, there probably was no better way to find out the things I wanted to know. I visited the clinics associated with the Palmer College of Chiropractic, Davenport, Iowa, and the National College of Chiropractic, Lombard, Illinois. These are regarded with pride in the chiropractic world as offering excellent treatment and care. At both I said that I was experiencing symptoms that are usually associated with the presence of certain serious conditions. The clinics' response made me wonder if I were Alice and had fallen down the rabbit hole.

First of all, I wanted to see for myself if today's chiropractors are really taught to treat disease according to the theories and techniques expounded almost seventy-five years ago by Daniel David Palmer.

Second, I was interested in the host of questions arising from that theory, some of which were touched on in the previous chapter. Is it true that the chiropractor is taught not to diagnose the symptoms that his patients present but simply to adjust the spine? If a patient went to a chiropractor with symptoms of a serious condition, would the chiropractor recognize the symptoms as indicating the possible presence of that condition? Would he try to discover whether or not the patient had that illness? I need hardly be said that, for innumerable persons who seek health care from chiropractors, the answer to this question involves the difference between sickness and health, between recovery and disability, and even between life and death.

I also wanted to know how chiropractors would react to a spine in which recognized medical specialists and roentgenologists could find no significant abnormality. Would chiropractors find subluxations in such a spine that they regarded as being serious enough to cause illness?

The clinics of the Palmer and National colleges seemed good places to make the test. In both, the actual clinic work is done by senior students or recent graduates, and their methods would therefore reflect present-day teaching at leading colleges of chiropractic. At the same time, each case handled at these clinics is reviewed and supervised by chiropractors on the faculties of the colleges and the staffs of the clinics, who are recognized as skilled leaders of the profession. The analysis of my condition and the treatment I would receive, therefore, would bear the stamp of approval of prominent and experienced chiropractors.

Since Palmer and its clinic are affiliated with the

"straights," and National and its clinic are affiliated with the "mixers," I would have an opportunity to try both types of treatment and discover if the differences in theory which have split the chiropractic world down the middle reveal themselves in the therapies that the two groups offer.

Because Palmer is a "straight" college, and its students devote their attention largely or exclusively to the spine as the cause of disease, I decided to present at the Palmer Clinic the symptoms of a straightforward back problem —a disc lesion, or, in laymen's language, a slipped, compressed, or damaged disc.

At National Clinic, I decided to present the symptoms of angina pectoris—coronary artery disease. I not only wanted to see if they would recognize the symptoms of this lethal condition, but I wanted to see how the "mixer" philosophy would react to a malady that could not conceivably originate in the spine.

As recent experiences with human heart transplants have shown, this organ can function perfectly without the help of the nervous system. "The origin of the heartbeat is in the muscle and the heart will beat in the absence of any nervous connection," says Hyman S. Mayerson, Ph.D., professor of physiology and chairman of the department of physiology at Tulane University Medical School. Furthermore, heart trouble is primarily heart muscle trouble, whether the cause is disease of the muscle fibers or faulty coronary artery circulation. Heart trouble, therefore, could not possibly be treated by "relieving spinal nerve pressure" even if such pressure really existed.

First, I went to one of the nation's best urban hospitals and had the most exhaustive physical examination that I have ever undergone. It included fourteen different laboratory tests, an electrocardiogram, and an especially detailed study of my spine, based on a series of X-ray plates taken from every angle.

Apart from the fact that I have, and have had for many years, several small, benign sebaceous cysts, this examination failed to reveal any deviation from normal health. The physician supervising the examination wrote to me:

> The physical examination was entirely within normal limits and there were no significant abnormal findings except for several fibrous or cystic subcutaneous nodules on your face, your back, and your right thigh. The large battery of biochemical tests which were made the following day failed to disclose any abnormality. Your electrocardiogram is normal; the X ray of your chest demonstrated your heart and lungs to be normal in size and contour. You were particularly interested in the condition of your back and for that reason, X rays of the entire spinal column were made and these films failed to show any significant abnormality.

My first stop was the Palmer College in Davenport. The college occupies three city blocks on an attractive site at the top of a hill overlooking the Mississippi River. Across the street are the modern transmitting facilities of stations WOC and WOC-TV. One of the transmission towers is mounted atop the D. D. Palmer Memorial Building, a classroom facility on campus.

After browsing around the campus and viewing the two marble monuments to D. D. and B. J. Palmer, I entered the clinic building (a slogan on the steps said "Keep Smiling") and told the receptionist that I would like to see someone about a "back problem."

A student in a white coat promptly appeared, whom we will call Dr. Tom Blake (students working in the clinic wore name tags identifying them as "Dr." so-and-so). We shook hands and Dr. Blake led me into the clinic, a large open area divided up into some thirty treatment cubicles. The place was busy. There were patients in a number of the cubicles, and student chiropractors were scurrying around everywhere. Dr. Blake told me that last year the clinic handled some 28,000 patient-visits.

We entered a treatment cubicle and sat down. I asked

him if his work in the clinic was supervised, or if he was "on his own." He replied that his findings, recommendations, and plans for treatment in every case he handled were reviewed and approved by chiropractors on the faculty of the college and/or the staff of the clinic.

I then described my "symptoms" to him. I had, I said, an off-and-on back pain. Sometimes this pain was accompanied by pain extending through my hip, down the back of my right leg, past my knee, and almost as far as my ankle. The pain, I said, never entered my other leg, and never extended upward in my back.

This set of symptoms, I had been told by several physicians, would suggest the possible presence of a slipped or damaged disc in my back. Such symptoms should be carefully checked because the condition is serious. The usual treatment is bed rest on a hard bed, sometimes accompanied by traction. Disc lesions can rarely or never be helped by manipulation of the spine by hand. In fact, manipulation is usually contraindicated, since pushing and jerking the spine is likely to aggravate existing damage.

Dr. Blake took my medical history. I then removed my shirt and undershirt and sat with my back to him. He ran his fingers slowly and evenly down my back, then began to feel the vertebrae of my lower spine. "Finding anything?" I asked. "Yes," he said. "There are subluxations in there [pressing my lower spine] and there [touching a spot in my mid-back, just below where I told him that the pain stopped]." He then felt my neck, turned my head to the left and right, and stated that there was a third subluxation in my atlas, at the top of the spine where it joins the head.

I lay down on the chiropractic adjustment table in the cubicle and Dr. Blake went back over my lower spine. "There's edema [swelling] there," he told me.

I got up from the table and we arranged for me to have X rays taken at 6:45 that evening. We then conversed for a while. I evinced great interest in chiropractic

31

theory, and he obligingly explained it to me. Subluxations, he said, "cause the nerve impulses to go either too fast or too slow," causing the organs served by these haywire nerves to function incorrectly. This, he said, was the cause of disease.

I asked if chiropractic treatment was good for things other than back conditions. "Oh, yes," he replied. "One of our big problems is to dispel the public's belief that chiropractic treatment is for back troubles only." For example, he said, chiropractic adjustments can cure ulcers. They can also cure gallstones.

"What about a heart condition?" I asked.

"Yes," he replied, "if it's caught in time."

At 6:45 that evening I met Dr. Blake at the clinic and we went to the X-ray department in another building. He took two 14-by-36 inch "full spine" X rays, one from the front and one from the side. This is standard chiropractic practice. However, as we shall learn in Chapter Eight, it is unusual for medical roentgenologists to take such plates to analyze conditions in a specified area of the spine. A smaller plate carefully focused on the afflicted area not only yields far clearer and more detailed information, but exposes the patient to much less radiation.

When I returned to the clinic at 1 P.M. the next day Dr. Blake said that the X rays had been developed, and they confirmed his discovery of three subluxations. One was the fifth lumbar vertebra, the second was the ninth dorsal vertebra, and the third, as he had already stated, was the atlas.

We went into another treatment cubicle where, under the supervision of a senior student, we buckled down to the nitty-gritty.

For my first adjustment I lay down on a hard, flat couch, on my left side. Dr. Blake drew up my right leg, clasped it between his knees, bent over me, and placed his left hand in the small of my back and his right hand on my chest just below my right shoulder. Suddenly he gave a sharp thrust into my spine with his left hand and arm, using his right to keep me from slipping. There was some pain, but even more predominant was the sensation of shock—a swift and ruthless taking of the body by surprise, before it can marshal its defenses. I wondered what such a thrust would have done to a damaged disc if I had had one.*

The next adjustments were the ones described at the beginning of this chapter. They consisted of three heavy downward thrusts, one to adjust the supposed subluxation in my mid-back at the ninth dorsal, and two to adjust the fifth lumbar in the small of my back. It was at this latter spot that I experienced for about two weeks thereafter the soreness that one usually feels with a slightly pulled or strained back.

Dr. Blake then adjusted my atlas. I sat on a chair, and, standing behind me, he took my head in his hands and felt the area behind my ears carefully, pushing his fingers in firmly. He then rolled my head to the right and gave it a sudden jerk. This apparently did not produce the desired effect. The supervising student took Dr. Blake's place behind me and repeated the process, also apparently without success. My atlas, they agreed, was "very tight" on the right side.

Dr. Blake then resumed his place behind me, rotated my head to the left, and jerked it. I felt and heard a snap in my neck. This was apparently what they were seeking—they pronounced the left-side adjustment successful.

Back in our own treatment cubicle, Dr. Blake explained soberly that a subluxated atlas such as I had could pinch "the whole cord" and cause just about any kind of trouble.

I asked him what disease or condition I was suffering from. He replied that chiropractors do not seek to diagnose or identify illnesses; rather, they locate and remove the cause in the spine.

I asked him what types of conditions were treated at

---

* For the views of a leading specialist on this, see the comments of Dr. Solomon D. Winokur, p. 113.

the clinic, assuming that they had been diagnosed and identified elsewhere. "They run the gamut," he said. "You name it." He confided to me that they included patients who really had nothing wrong with them at all. The backs of these patients are adjusted, along with all the rest. "You don't often come across a back that doesn't have a subluxation," he said. As for actual illnesses, one of his current patients has sinus trouble. Other ailments that he had seen treated at the clinic included bursitis, ulcers, a malady that involved "spitting blood," headache, sciatica, and heart conditions.

As we parted Dr. Blake told me that subluxations are rarely or never put permanently back into place by a single adjustment, and that I should therefore continue treatment with a chiropractor back home. This, of course, meant that, if the subluxations existed, I would still have them when I visited the National College clinic.

The next day I presented myself at the National College clinic in Lombard, Illinois. However, they were booked solid for the rest of the day and could not take me. I made an appointment for 11:00 the following morning.

When I arrived for my appointment I was met by a young chiropractor—we'll call him Dr. John May. At National College, I found, the clinic work is done by recently graduated students, who work at the clinic for fifteen to eighteen weeks before beginning their practice. As is the case at Palmer, their work is supervised by chiropractors on the college faculty and on the staff of the clinic.

National College's buildings and clinic are somewhat more modern than Palmer's. Instead of the one large, gymnasium-like room sectioned off into cubicles by wall dividers, in which the Palmer clinic is housed, the National clinic has individual patient treatment rooms. We entered one, and I described my "symptoms."

For about a year, I said, I had been having dull, cramplike pains in my chest. I had them sometimes two or three times a day, sometimes only once a week. They tended to come when I had been exerting myself heavily, or when I was angry or under strong emotional stress. The pains, I continued, would cause me to breathe deeply. They lasted for periods of time ranging from a few seconds to a few minutes. When they came, I said, they would go away if I simply stopped what I was doing—or, if they came when I was angry, they would go away if I just took it easy, sat back, and relaxed. I added that these pains would sometimes go up from my chest into my left shoulder and arm.

These symptoms, physicians told me, clearly suggest the possible presence of a coronary heart condition. I even helped Dr. May along by saying pointedly that the pains were never in my back, thus making it unlikely that my condition was arthritis.

Dr. May asked me no questions about my symptoms, and showed not the slightest sign of recognizing their possible significance. He took a brief medical history. As he finished it, Dr. Eugene V. Hoffmann, Jr., a chiropractor who is an assistant director of the clinic, came in. Dr. May told him that I had "dull chest pains, going up into his left shoulder and arm." Dr. Hoffmann was apparently as impervious to the possible meaning of the symptoms as Dr. May. He asked me no questions.

I took my shirt off and Dr. Hoffmann, the assistant clinic director, felt my upper left shoulder and my spine. He told me that the musculature of my left side was more developed than that of my right, and that that might well be causing my trouble. I told him that I was right-handed. He replied that perhaps my left-side musculature had nevertheless become overdeveloped by such activities as lifting.

He then felt my neck, pushing his fingers in firmly and asking me if it were tender. I said no. Dr. Hoffmann then turned things over to Dr. May, and left the room. Dr. May took me in front of a mirror to show me that my left shoulder was higher than my right. In the mirror, it was clearly not so. "It shows when you sit down," he said.

We then went to another room, where I lay face down

35

on a chiropractic adjustment table. Dr. May put a hot compress on my back "to relax" my spine, and left me there for about ten minutes. In the next room I heard a man gasping in pain as he was adjusted.

Dr. May re-entered the room, removed the compress, felt my neck and back, and settled his hands upon the area just below my shoulder blades. "Finding anything?" I asked. "Yes," he said, "you have a subluxation there." "Where is it?" I asked. "At the fifth dorsal," he replied. He found nothing at the ninth dorsal or the fifth lumbar, where the Palmer clinic had told me I had subluxations. Conversely, Palmer had found nothing at the fifth dorsal.

Dr. May gave a sharp thrust at the fifth dorsal, and my spine popped audibly. Next he moved to the bottom of my spine. "One down there?" I asked. "Your hips are slightly out of line," he replied, and gave me a wingding adjustment. He then took my head and jerked it left and right, getting a good sharp pop each time.

That concluded the treatment. I sat up and asked him if the subluxation at the fifth dorsal might be causing my chest pains. He replied that nerves lead from the fifth dorsal to "organs all around the chest area," and the subluxation there might well be causing my pain.

As was the case at Palmer, he told me that a series of adjustments would be necessary to get my subluxated vertebra permanently back into place. I asked him if X ray of my spine would be advisable to establish that it was indeed subluxated. He said that it was not necessary.

I had intended to continue my research by offering myself as a guinea pig in the office of individual chiropractors. But as I left the clinic and got into my car I felt a sharp twinge from my lower-back adjustments at Palmer. I couldn't help remembering the comment made by Dr. Edward T. Wentworth, past president of the Medical Society of the State of New York: "Only a strong, healthy person can afford to indulge in chiropractic treatment." My back had been healthy before I began the project, and I decided there was no point in taking further risk.

Another consideration prevented me from making further tests—the frequent use of X ray by many chiropractors. Although the National Clinic had not X-rayed me, I felt that I would be fortunate to escape from the office of the average chiropractor in private practice without getting a heavy dose of radiation, no matter what symptoms I presented. That was one of the many things I had learned when, posing as a chiropractor, I attended a three-day seminar in practice-building given by the Parker Chiropractic Research Foundation in the fall of 1967.

CHAPTER FOUR

The Supersalesmen

JAMES W. PARKER IS ONE OF THE MOST SUCCESSFUL CHIRO-practors in the United States—a shrewd, earthy man, a born storyteller, and a person of tireless energy. He has the revivalist preacher's gift for holding an audience for hours, permitting his voice to gain in speed and rise in pitch and dramatic intensity, then suddenly lowering it to make a point, start another subject, or tell an unexpected deadpan joke.

Parker has the King Midas touch. The creator of a chain of eighteen thriving chiropractic clinics in Texas, he has grossed millions of dollars while spending over half a million on advertising and public relations. After making one fortune from treating ill persons he is making another from his fellow chiropractors. His project seems to be nothing less than turning the entire chiropractic profession into an army of smooth-talking, wheeling-and-dealing supersalesmen.

Parker has set up an operation called the Parker School of Professional Success. This, in turn, is a division of another Parker creation, the Parker Chiropractic Research

Foundation. The name of this latter organization appears on diplomas issued by the school.

Finally, there is a third organization, Share International, which uses the offices and personnel of the other two. Share International is the sales arm of the operation, providing chiropractors with materials for putting the Parker system into operation in their own practice. It issues a mail-order catalog, and also sets up shop and sells its wares during the three-day seminars in "practice building" that Parker holds six times a year, usually at the headquarters of the three enterprises in the Hotel Texas in Fort Worth. Six thousand chiropractors and their assistants have attended one or more of the seminars, and more flock to Fort Worth as each new one is held.

The fee for attending the three-day course is $250. I sent it in, calling myself "Dr. Lee Smith, Chiropractor." There are directories of licensed chiropractors, and I am not listed in them since I am not a chiropractor. But my registration was accepted without question.

When I checked in at the seminar registration desk in the Hotel Texas an attractive girl smiled and handed me a handsome split cowhide briefcase with "Dr. Lee Smith" stamped on the side in gold. Inside was a sample packet of materials available from Share International, and a 336-page multigraphed soft-cover book called *Textbook of Office Procedure and Practice Building for the Chiropractic Profession*. The seminar, I soon learned, is built around this remarkable book.

Over two hundred chiropractors and their assistants were in attendance when Parker, a man of medium height with black hair, a burr haircut, black horn-rimmed glasses, and a neat small mustache, wearing a badge that said simply "Dr. Jim," stepped to the rostrum to begin the first session at 1 P.M. "At these sessions," he said, "I intend to teach you all the gimmicks, gadgets, and gizmos that can be used to get new patients. . . . Thinking, feeling, acting determine the amount of money you will take to the bank. . . . Remember, enthusiasm is the yeast that raises the dough."

40

The afternoon and evening sessions were devoted to "Success Philosophy." It turned out that, when it comes to love, the hippies have nothing on Jim Parker. In order to succeed, the *Textbook* says, the chiropractor must "LLL: Lather Love Lavishly!!" "When you meet a new patient," Parker explained, "you can push a button. You can push the LLL button, the love button. It's like a light bulb that you switch on. When you meet a new patient, LLL him in. When you do this, you disarm a patient who has developed sales resistance."

However, like the hippies, Parker finds some people more lovable than others. An unlovable type from the chiropractor's point of view is a person with an acute illness. The course, says the *Textbook*, "is designed to make you a 'D.C.'—'Doctor of Chronics' rather than a Doctor of Acutes." "You'll make a lot more money," Parker explained.

But what if the patient comes in with acute, rather than chronic, symptoms? The chiropractor's task, Parker said, is to try to discover that the symptoms are "an acute flareup of a chronic condition," and to convince the patient that this is so.

During this and succeeding sessions many subjects were covered, including: how to advertise for patients (chiropractors can buy mats for whole series of newspaper ads from Share International); how to get patients to refer other patients; how to answer the questions of people who doubt the validity of chiropractic treatment (a dual technique is used—frightening people away from scientific medical treatment by alleging that its methods are "deadly," and claiming that such treatment, with all its dangers, deals only with "the symptoms" of disease while chiropractic attacks and eliminates the "true cause"); when to give presents to patients and their children and what to give; how to arrange the office suite ("place Bible in reception room"); how to maintain a mailing list and what literature to send.

Perhaps the most important topic, however, was the basic procedure for getting the patient into treatment.

41

As the *Textbook* neatly summarized it: "From the time the telephone rings until the time you start the examination, you are working toward one goal: 'Mr. Jones, there is most definitely something wrong with your spine that could absolutely be causing almost all, if not every bit, of your trouble.'"

The *Textbook* kicks off the subject with a detailed discussion of telephone technique, including many sample conversations. "If possible," it says, "the assistant should handle calls since she can refuse requests for prices and can praise the doctor and chiropractic with an emphasis not possible for the doctor himself."

When the doctor does get on the line, his job is to get the prospect in. The bait on the hook is a "free consultation":

Q: "How much do you charge?"

A: "There is no charge . . . [pause] . . . for the consultation of the first visit. This is to determine the cause of your trouble and what should be done about it."

"Tact and diplomacy are necessary," the *Textbook* notes. "Such sentences as the following OPEN THE TRAP-DOOR":

". . . I certainly understand what you mean when you say you spent so much money without getting results. We will try hard not to let that happen when you come here."

". . . Your (nice/cultured) voice tells me you are an intelligent (woman/man) and I am sure once you have made up your mind to try something you will follow through."

Actually, the *Textbook* explains, the patient will *not* learn "the cause of your trouble and what should be done about it" in the free consultation. Its purpose is to get the caller into the doctor's office so he can make a complete selling pitch in person. "The consultation is without cost," says the book, "but the examination will cost them money."

When the patient comes in, the chiropractor's assistant first secures basic information including name and address. The doctor should "check the patient's address for income status" (later on the doctor is also to "learn family occupation by developing interest in the family. This should be done subtly"). The patient is then ushered into the august presence, where the doctor deals with him in a thirteen-step procedure that leaves nothing to chance.

As the unsuspecting patient enters, the doctor pushes the love button and lathers him lavishly. While the lather flows the doctor seeks to "establish common bond" through such links as "fraternal jewelry, children, similar religious affiliations."

"What would you like me to do for you?" he then asks. His moves now, according to the *Textbook*, are:

(1) Eye contact.
(2) Lean forward.
(3) Hands on desk, or one hand on edge of desk and other at side.
(4) When patient begins to answer, you can lean back in chair and listen attentively with arms and legs uncrossed.

Now come the most important steps. First, the "Yet Disease." "If the patient has a pain in his left shoulder," Dr. Parker said, "ask, 'Has the pain started in your right shoulder yet?' Use it when you must instill a sufficient amount of fear to get the patient to take chiropractic."

The next step is to "dig for chronicity." The doctor puts an elaborate series of questions to the patient that suggest or imply that the condition is chronic. "How long has it been since you really felt good?" the doctor murmurs gently. ("I make $10,000 a year on that one, easy," a chiropractor sitting next to me whispered in my ear.)

With the verbal digging completed and chronicity unearthed, the chiropractor moves on to "Connect up affected parts (pain) with the area of treatment (spine)"— that is, to tell the patient that his condition stems from spinal subluxations. Having done this, the chiropractor

43

is then to "restate information (or acquire additional information) which may prove useful later on to explain limited results, or to excuse you from getting result expected." As a final step he releases some more lather to "establish LLL principle in patient's mind." At this point says the *Textbook*, "most patients are ready to proceed."

With the fish on the line, the doctor is told to "lean back," make "eye contact," and reel him in with a speech that Parker calls "the assumptive close." It goes like this:

"Mr. Jones, at this point we can be sure of one thing—if you are not a chiropractic case, chiropractic will never help you. If you are a chiropractic case, nothing else will ever help you, so our first job is to determine whether or not you are a chiropractic case. We have had a number of similar cases in the past, and have found that the first thing to do is conduct a thorough (chiropractic) examination, including X rays, laboratory tests, a physical examination, orthopedic and neurological tests, and whatever else might be indicated, depending upon what we find. If you are ready, we can begin your examination right now" OR "When would you like to start this examination?" OR "Come with me."

If the fish wriggles, the chiropractor plays him carefully. The *Textbook* provides answers the chiropractor can give to every imaginable patient objection or reservation.

If the patient is still balky, the chiropractor offers a "preliminary examination." Beginning where the patient feels pain, he touches the afflicted parts, then says something like, "There doesn't seem to be anything wrong with the arm itself . . . let's trace the nerves back to the spine and check there." When this has been done, Dr. Parker suggested that the chiropractor can say, "Oh, here it is. Why didn't we look here first? I'm glad we found the trouble here, because this is my specialty." During the process, said Dr. Parker, the chiropractor can "ask leading questions" and "use little comments, innuendoes, such as 'Hmm. I don't like that.'"

Now the chiropractor pulls out all the stops. "Build fear of more serious trouble, if necessary," the book says. ". . . Proceed to make a serious statement followed by a hopeful statement, which would cover the full scale of patient feeling and emotion, as follows: 'Mrs. Brown, it's possible this could be the beginning of something serious. Let's see if chiropractic can help. It wouldn't make you mad if we stopped this pain/made a new back for you, would it?'"

If Mrs. Brown still doesn't see what is good for her, she gets both barrels between the eyes. "Do you feel there could be a tumor or perhaps cancer causing these nerves to act up?" the chiropractor asks. Having raised such specters, the chiropractor sits back and lets Mrs. Brown's fears do the rest. "Put the problem of making these decisions on the patient's shoulders," the book says.

No human extremity is out of bounds for the sales pitch. "In terminal cases," the book states, "mention 'a miracle of nature has often occurred.'"

While tightening the screws the chiropractor simultaneously keeps a sharp eye peeled for "the green light." Sooner or later, the book says, it comes.

The netted fish is then examined and X-rayed. In talking to the prospect on the phone before he comes in, the assistant is told, "Do not say the doctor is taking X rays or is in the darkroom. This may suggest that the caller will need X rays." If the patient puts the question to the doctor himself on the phone, the *Textbook* suggests various answers:

Q: Do I have to be X-rayed?
A: No, not necessarily. That depends upon what I find necessary after the consultation, for which there is no charge. What seems to be your trouble?

or

45

We require X rays in cases that may be serious. What seems to be your trouble?

Actually, in the Parker system it's a rare customer who escapes without at least one panoramic dose of radiation from the shoulders down to the area of the genitalia. X rays, Dr. Parker said, should be given to "most patients that come into the office," and they should be the big 14-by-36 glamour photos, "if for no other reason than psychological."

"If people hesitate about chiropractic X rays," Dr. Parker told the seminar, "compare them to dental X rays, and say that the spine is much more important." If the patient's spine has already been X-rayed in the course of established medical treatment and found to have no defects, he may wonder why it needs to be done again. The never-failing *Textbook* provides the chiropractor with his answer:

Q: My medical doctor has taken X rays and says there is nothing wrong with my spine.
A: He was looking for dislocation, luxations, fractures, ruptured discs, etc. We look for misalignments, curvatures, subluxations, thin cartilage, rotated or unbalanced hips and other conditions, any of which may be causing pressure on nerves, pain, distortions or other bodily abnormalities.

The *Textbook* also provides a note in parentheses: "Less patient resistance will be found if you say, 'Let's take some pictures' rather than 'Let's take X rays.'"

If the patient is actively worried about radiation he should be soothed: "If you were to have X rays taken once a month for an entire year, your life might be shortened as little as two days. Your overweight condition and your smoking are shortening your life hundreds of times more than could the small amount of radiation involved in the few pictures I need of your spine."

The word "little" in that first sentence should win any contest for the Sleeper of the Year.*

When the examination is completed, the doctor is told to collect for it on the spot. "That will be $27.50 for today," he is told to say. "Will that be cash or check?" "Begin writing receipt," the book continues. "Don't look up."

The *Textbook* covers the matter of the financial transaction with characteristic thoroughness. Every conceivable patient objection to immediate payment is foreseen and forestalled:

Q: I would give you a check but I don't have my checkbook with me.

A: I understand (smiling). Why don't you use one of our counter checks? Which bank do you use? (Complete the check and hand it to the patient for signature.)

. . .

Q: Just bill me.

A: I'm sorry, Mrs. Brown. It is customary to take care of X rays and examination at the time they are made.

. . .

Q: I didn't bring that much with me.

A: I understand. You may make a partial payment and take care of the rest tomorrow. Could you pay, say, $15 today? $10? $5? How much *can* you pay today?

. . .

Q: That certainly seems high.

A: Yes, it does, doesn't it? Things certainly are high these days. (Then make an analogy to the cost of your equipment, dental work, etc.)

To take care of cases in which the chiropractor has unwisely extended credit, he can purchase from Share

---

* For a discussion of the dangers of chiropractic X ray, see Chapter Eight.

International a handsome wall certificate stating that he is a member of the "State Credit Association," and a bookful of collection forms of graduated degrees of severity and threat, all bearing the heading "State Credit Association." No address for this credit association is given on either the wall certificate or the forms, and the forms all say "'MAKE YOUR PAYMENTS DIRECT TO THE CREDITOR." It is, of course, the chiropractor himself who mails them out.

On the patient's next visit the chiropractor hands the patient a document entitled *Confidential Report of Chiropractic Examination and Recommendations,* which consists of six sheets and a blue cover. Chiropractors purchase them from Share International. "Our examination has now been completed," it says. ". . . in your particular case, we have found definite misalignments in your SPINE resulting in a disturbed nervous system. Therefore, you are a case for chiropractic."

The *Report* explains the chiropractic theory of disease, and adds that "'the nervous system is the master system which controls all other systems of the entire body, including the glandular, reproductive, digestive, eliminative, respiratory, and circulatory." "They couldn't possibly have a condition not covered here," Dr. Parker observed.

The *Report* sets forth the chiropractor's "analysis" of the patient's illness ("analysis" was a word frequently used in the seminar; some states do not permit chiropractors to "diagnose" illness), together with a recommended number of visits for adjustments, a price for the series, and an offer of a discount if the patient pays the full sum in advance.

The *Textbook* adds some comments intended for the chiropractor's eyes only. "You might suggest only as many adjustments as the patient can pay for," it says. ". . . One adjustment for each year of age of the average chronic patient over twenty years of age is a rough thumbnail guide of what people will willingly accept and pay for." However, the book observes, there is no reason for the chiropractor to be unduly modest in his expectations:

"Chiropractors should keep in mind that many truck drivers, carpenters, electricians, steel workers, and radio repairmen earn more than $12,000 annually."

With the patient in treatment a new phase begins—"Patient Management." The emphasis is on causing the patient to believe that he is getting better, and getting him to say so.

On the first visit, the chiropractor is instructed to say, "Your spine is certainly rigid, but that adjustment took well."

From then on, through the first ten visits, the doctor is to greet the patient with the words, "What's better?" followed by some appropriate comment. For instance, on the second adjustment, the *Textbook* says, "If patient states that nothing is better and restates his trouble, say, 'Yes, I know; that's on your patient record card, but the adjustment took so well yesterday some improvement should have been noticed. Think hard now . . . isn't something better?' If patient tells of conditions that are better, say, 'Wonderful! Great! Good for you! I'm proud of you! I appreciate your getting well.'"

The recommended statements for adjustments three through ten are as follows:

Third adjustment: "What's better? Your eyes are brighter."

Fourth adjustment: "What's better? I hope you're feeling as good as you look."

Fifth adjustment: "What's better? You're getting a spring in your step."

Sixth adjustment: "What's better? You're getting in fightin' trim."

Seventh adjustment: "What's better? Your body and mind are getting more rest in each hour that you sleep than ever before."

Eighth adjustment: "What's better? Did you know you'll live longer as a result of these adjustments?"

Ninth adjustment: "What's better? Did you know you'll have fewer colds, sore throats, etc., as a result of these adjustments?"

Tenth adjustment: "What's better? Did you know you'll do better work during the time you are having these adjustments?"

As the treatment proceeds, the chiropractor moves on to the next step—he begins to pump the patient for names of possible prospects. "Repeat 'common bond' procedure," the book says, "and subtly question patient about friends, neighbors, and relatives who may be in need of chiropractic." Names can even be gotten from patients who are not feeling improvement. "To get new names from non-responding patients," says the text, "say, 'if other illnesses in your family are worrying you, it will slow down your response. How is everyone in your family?'" Patients and others should be told to "Remind your friends that chiropractic is good for practically *all* diseases."

When the patient comes up with names, the chiropractor records them in a prospect list and goes after them. The procedure involves the mailing of special literature, personal letters (suggested wording supplied in the *Textbook*), and even phone calls. If the prospect responds with interest he is offered a "free consultation" and the cycle is repeated.

Throughout the procedure the chiropractor tries to wean the patient away from established medical treatment—permanently, if possible. "A true chiropractic patient," says the *Textbook,* "is one whose convictions with regard to health have been diverted from the muddy road of medicine to the superhighway of chiropractic by a series of correlated mental concepts, positively implanted in proper order."

As for the chiropractor, there is at least one concept of which *he* should never lose sight: the "Money Concept." It doesn't even hurt, the *Textbook* indicates, to let the world know that this concept interests you. "Carry $100 bill in billfold," it advises, and "write $$$$$ and big amounts."

After the three days of seminar sessions, members attended a farewell dinner. Dr. Parker gave each of us a handsome diploma from the Parker Chiropractic Research Foundation, stating that we had "completed the prescribed course of study at the Parker Chiropractic Research Seminar" (actually, no one was required to "complete" anything, since no attendance was taken at any of the sessions). Those wishing to do so could also join the Foundation for $10 a year and receive a second item—an impressive black-and-silver membership plaque "similar to the plaque of the American Academy of Reconstructive Surgery [Plastic Surgeons], who are about the highest in prestige of any group of specialists anywhere."

I talked to many chiropractors during the three-day period. Their response to the seminar was overwhelmingly enthusiastic. Over half those in attendance wore blue badges showing that they had attended previous seminars and had come back for more. A chiropractor from Ohio told me that he had been attending the seminars since 1959; by applying Parker's methods he had built his practice from $25,000 to $100,000 a year. Another said that this was his eighteenth seminar. "After the first one my income went up from $2,000 to $4,000 a month," he said. He is also now near the $100,000 mark. A third didn't give figures but summarized his situation with graphic simplicity. "We have gone," he said, "from rags to riches."

While he learns to travel this upward path, his receptionist in his office back home—if she is following the recommendations of the *Textbook*—is telling patients and callers that "Dr. _____ is doing some graduate work in Fort Worth."

During intervals in the seminar sessions I browsed in the Share International display center in the room adjoining the seminar hall. Immense amounts of material were available and chiropractors were hauling it off by the shopping-basketful. One item was a small device called a "Thermeter," a meter with a needle, contained in a handheld circular metal housing from which two prongs protruded. It cost $79.95. Chiropractors who were standing around the display with me explained that the two prongs are applied to the spine, and the device is run up and down the backbone. Especially sharp deflections of the needle indicate the pattern of subluxations.

As we shall see in the next chapter, many chiropractors love gadgets.

CHAPTER FIVE

The
Gadgeteers

On May 24, 1963, Mrs. Jackie Metcalf, a twenty-two-year-old Torrance, California, housewife, mounted the steps of a white, one-story building on LaBrea Avenue in Los Angeles and entered a door marked "Dr. Ruth B. Drown, Chiropractor." Inside she gave three small pieces of blotting paper to Dr. Drown and her daughter, Dr. Cynthia Chatfield, also a chiropractor. The stains on the blotters, Mrs. Metcalf said, were samples of blood from her three children. She asked to have her children's ills diagnosed from the blood samples and paid $50 for each diagnosis.

She later testified that in a few days she heard from Dr. Chatfield that analysis of the blood samples showed the youngsters to be coming down with chicken pox and mumps. On an earlier visit Mrs. Metcalf had purchased a "little black box"—a $588 Drown Therapeutic Instrument—to treat herself and her family at home. Dr. Chatfield, she said, told her how to set the dials on the machine to cure the children.

Mrs. Metcalf, however, was not just another patient—

she was an undercover agent for the California State Department of Public Health. Her three children were not ill. And the blood samples she gave to Doctors Drown and Chatfield were not her children's blood—they were the blood of a turkey, a sheep, and a pig.

On the basis of this and other evidence, Los Angeles County Deputy District Attorney John W. Miner—the prosecutor in the Marvin Phillips murder case—swooped down on the LaBrea Avenue building with a squad of police and public health inspectors, arrested Doctors Drown and Chatfield and an assistant, Mrs. Margaret Lunness, and took into custody enough Alice-in-Wonderland machines to fill a wing of the Smithsonian Institution. Dr. Drown died in 1965 while awaiting trial. Dr. Chatfield and Mrs. Lunness were convicted of grand theft for their part of the operation and in 1967 were sentenced—Mrs. Lunness being placed on probation for three years and Dr. Chatfield receiving an indefinite prison term. They are presently appealing the convictions.*

Ruth B. Drown and Cynthia Chatfield gave conventional chiropractic adjustments to their patients. They also did a lot more. They epitomized two notable tendencies among many chiropractors—love of pseudo-scientific gadgetry, and a weakness for foolish and dangerous medical theories.

At the time of Dr. Drown's arrest she had treated 35,000 persons from all over the country with her diagnostic and therapeutic gadgets, and had sold the devices to other parties who had treated an unknown number of other patients. The devices could allegedly diagnose and cure nearly every known affliction from jealousy to cancer, plus a few ailments such as "extra kidney" which Dr.

---

* The information in this chapter on the Drown treatment and the Drown Laboratories operation is based on testimony at this trial, *People* v. *Chatfield and Lunness*, no. 279660, Super. Ct. Cal., L. A. Co. 1966, and an earlier Federal trial, *Drown* v. *U.S.*, 198 F 2d. 999 (9 Cir 1952), Cert. Den. 344 U.S. 920 (1953), mentioned below.

Drown described as "not unusual" but which medical science has yet to discover. Actually, expert witnesses testified that the elaborate machines that form the basis of the Drown treatment are a hoax. The judge stated that the theory of the treatment is totally invalid.

Ruth Drown got some of her ideas from Dr. Albert Abrams, king of twentieth-century gadget quacks, who died in 1924 after having made millions selling his machines and treating patients with them. According to the Abrams theory, which he called "radionics," all parts of the body vibrate and emit electrical impulses of different, ascertainable frequencies. What's more, diseased organs emit impulses of different frequencies from healthy ones. To diagnose illness one "tuned in" on the body's organs with an Abrams radionics machine, noted where abnormal vibrations were occurring, and pinpointed the nature of the illness from the rate of vibration. The "cure" consisted in allegedly feeding proper vibrations into the body with an Abrams machine, thus overcoming the improper ones.

The Abrams contraptions inspired numerous imitations —perhaps as many as fifty. In state and federal legal actions against such devices, experts have repeatedly testified that both the machines and the theory behind them are sheer nonsense. This did not deter Ruth Drown, who took the old master's notions and added many imaginative twists of her own.

At Drown Laboratories a patient was told to sit beside an impressive console and put his feet on two footpads made of German silver. The console had nine knobs arranged in three rows of three, and each knob had settings numbered from zero through ten. On the console panel there was also an ammeter. Near the right-hand corner of the desk on which the console was mounted was a small rectangular rubber membrane clamped down by a metal frame. Next to this was a cylindrical depression about an inch-and-a-half deep.

Seated at the console, Dr. Drown placed an electrode made of lead on some portion of the patient's body, usually his abdomen. This immediately caused a movement of the needle on the ammeter. With her right middle finger, on which she wore a rubber covering, Dr. Drown then stroked the rubber membrane while making adjustments on the nine dials with her left hand. When her finger began to "stick" or squeak on the rubber, this indicated that the dial settings were beginning to approach the vibration rate of the part or organ of the body that she was supposedly testing.

Next she would open a drawer of her desk and draw forth a number of sealed glass vials, each containing a different chemical. These she would insert, unopened, into the depression in the desk, one by one, while continuing to make careful adjustments on the dials. By this means she supposedly arrived at the exact vibration rate. She would then read off the numbers at which the dials were set, beginning with the upper left dial and proceeding horizontally across the three rows to the lower right. This composite number, taken down by an assistant on a large chart, represented the vibration rate of the illness, which could be looked up in an immense "rate book."

The "rate book" also indicated the "normal" vibration rate, to be fed back into the body to restore health. In treatment the patient lay down in a small cubicle in the Drown Laboratories, placed his feet against footpads, and applied a lead electrode to the area designated by Dr. Drown. Wires led from the footpads and the electrode to a Drown treatment machine in another room, which was essentially the same as a diagnostic machine except that it had no rubber plate. The nine dials of the treatment machine were set to the numbers indicated in the rate book and the patient supposedly received healing vibrations of just the right frequency.

Another Drown treatment device was a tremendous hollow coil into which the patient, lying on a slab, was bodily inserted. "All we know about it," Dr. Drown told investigators, "is that a coil with a charge in it seems to straighten up people who walk lopsided." State officials who impounded the device at the time of the arrests promptly dubbed it "The Tunnel of Love."

If a patient wished to do so he could buy a nine-dial treatment machine for home use. After being diagnosed at the laboratory the patient would be told where to set the dials for regular treatment sessions at home.

But even this was only the beginning. If a patient didn't want to bother being hooked up to a machine, either at the laboratories or at home, he didn't have to. Doctors Drown and Chatfield kept dried specimens of each patient's blood on pieces of blotting paper. If a patient felt ill he could call Drown Laboratories, and the blood sample would be inserted into a slot in the diagnostic machine. The blood sample supposedly remained in some kind of continuous communication with the rest of the patient's blood, wherever he might be, and thus reflected any current illness.

Treatment, too, could be "indirect." For $35 a month Drown Laboratories would insert the patient's blood specimen into a treatment machine at a specified time each day, set the dials to the indicated healing rate, and broadcast an hour's worth of treatment to the patient, which would supposedly reach him anywhere on the face of the earth.

Ruth Drown also claimed that her machines could take photographs of the diseased organs of patients, wherever the patients were. She called the process "radio-vision." Several such photographs were exhibited at the trial, including one allegedly taken by a Drown machine in London showing a blood clot and cancer in a patient in Connecticut. One medical expert called it "completely unintelligible"; another said that it looked to him like a Rorschach inkblot.

Dr. Drown had lots of other ideas. One of them was that jazz music was a cause of cancer. Cancer caused by jazz, she said, could be dissipated by playing such soothing tunes as Carrie Jacobs Bond's "Perfect Day."

She also believed that each human body is surrounded by a magnetic field, and that people should be taught how to care for their magnetic fields properly. One of her publications, the *Drown Atlas of Radio Therapy*, says,

> . . . Any patient who is weak and depleted should never take shower baths and stand in the water over the drain, because the patient's magnetism is washed down with the water through the drain, leaving him depleted. Also, a weak patient, after having had a tub bath, should leave the tub and have someone else drain the water and clean the tub. If it is necessary to do this himself, he should leave the tub and put on a robe before starting to drain the tub. Too many people sit in the tub and drain the water while finishing the bath, and their own magnetism is drained through the drain pipes to the ground, leaving the patient with that much less reserve.

As early as 1949 the Drown devices had been shown completely incapable of diagnosing illness. At a University of Chicago experiment Dr. Drown was supplied with blood samples of a number of persons and asked to diagnose their conditions. In one case, after working over her dials for an hour, she announced that the patient had cancer of the left breast which had spread to the ovaries, uterus, pancreas, gall bladder, spleen, and kidney; that she was blind in her right eye; that her ovaries were not functioning properly; and that there was reduced function of various organs including the stomach, spinal nerves, and heart. Actually, the patient was suffering from tuberculosis of the upper lobe of the right lung.

In 1951 Dr. Drown was tried on federal charges of introducing a misbranded device in interstate commerce. At the trial one of the government's expert witnesses, Dr. Elmer Belt, described the Drown device as "perfectly useless." "You just do not seem to think much of the instrument, do you, Dr. Belt?" the defense attorney asked. "I couldn't even use it to amuse the children," Dr. Belt replied. Dr. Drown was found guilty by the jury and was fined $1,000. She stopped shipping her devices across state lines but otherwise carried on business as usual.

In 1966 Dr. Chatfield and Mrs. Lunness went to trial in Los Angeles on the state charges. In addition to receiving Mrs. Jackie Metcalf's firsthand account, the court heard a procession of witnesses relate astounding stories. One testified that Dr. Drown assured him that his son, a diabetic, could reduce his intake of insulin, prescribed by a doctor, if he took the Drown treatment. Another witness, an epileptic, was told by Dr. Drown that she could cure him; she said that he would be able to stop taking the drug dilantin prescribed by his physician, and she continued to treat him even after he had a severe seizure in her office. In another case a chiropractor who used Drown therapy instruments on his patients brought a man to Drown Laboratories who had polyps in his lower intestinal tract. A diagnosis by Drown instruments showed no cancer, and the chiropractor therefore continued to treat the supposedly benign polyps with a Drown therapy device. The patient's condition worsened; a biopsy, done by a medical doctor, showed the growths to be malignant; and the patient died.

A dramatic highlight of the trial was the testimony of Dr. Moses A. Greenfield, professor of radiology at the UCLA School of Medicine and a consultant to the Atomic Energy Commission. Disassembling a Drown device in open court, Dr. Greenfield explained that all it basically consisted of was a length of wire linking together two pieces of dissimilar metal—the German silver of the footpads and the lead of the electrode. The only function performed by the patient was to complete the otherwise broken circuit. With the circuit complete, a small electric current flowed between the two metals, which registered on the ammeter on the console. The entire device therefore operated like a simple flashlight battery. It was even possible to eliminate the patient entirely. Dr. Greenfield demonstrated that the same deflection of the ammeter needle could be produced by dipping the footpad and electrode into a dish of water instead of applying them to a human body.

As for the nine dials with their ten numbered settings, Dr. Greenfield dismounted the panel and showed that only two wires connected each dial to the circuit. Further dismantling showed that the ten positions of each switch were connected together and it therefore made no difference in which position any of the dials was set.

The Drown case demonstrated that leadership in nonsense in chiropractic comes from some of the field's luminaries and educators. Ruth Drown had been president of the Drown College of Chiropractic. Raymond H. Houser, former dean of the Los Angeles College of Chiropractic, testified at the trial that he had used the Drown device for treatment.

With the Drown-Chatfield operation out of business, I wondered if any other chiropractors were treating patients without seeing them. In the spring of 1968 I found one in the Midwest, whom we shall call Dr. Johnson.

Dr. Johnson, I was told, diagnosed patients by mail, using specimens of their saliva. I therefore went to a biomedical laboratory and obtained, on a piece of typing paper, a specimen of the saliva of a female goat. I sent this to Dr. Johnson with the following letter:

Dear Dr. Johnson,

My firend from Chicago who have your treatment find it very helpful, and I write to ask your help. He send specimen of salava, and you tell him of his ailments and send him pills and he is feeling much better.

I am 40 years old, five feet 10 in. tall, weigh 150. Do not always feel well and some days are bad, like today. But do not know the cause. I enclose paper with my salava and hope you can help. If this is wrong way to do specimen please tell me. Pains sometimes severe. Thank you and ablige.

Sincerely yours.

As it turned out, I *had* done it the wrong way. Dr. Johnson replied promptly, saying, "To make these tests we need specially demagnetized paper, which I am sending you." The fee, he noted, was $20.

Not having time to return to the biomedical laboratory, I took the slip of "demagnetized" paper to a veterinary hospital, where a veterinarian placed upon it a specimen of the saliva of a happy, healthy black male dog named Steve, who had no illnesses or infirmities. I sent it to Dr. Johnson along with a $20 check.

Again his reply was prompt. "I have just completed a very careful test for you," he wrote in a letter dated two days after I mailed him the specimen and check from New York:

> I find—Acidosis—Arteriosclerosis—Heart strain—Malnutrition—Pellagra—Streptococcus infection in the bowel and as a result of that, you have pin worm. I am sending garlic to get rid of that.
>
> All glands and organs are low in function, for you are very badly run down.
>
> Gall bladder, kidneys, lymph glands, thyroid and prostate are the worst.
>
> Your body is starved for minerals.
>
> Eat all food as nearly God made it as is possible— not as man has ruined it.
>
> Three fourths of the "stuff" (it's not really food) in the Super Market is not fit to carry home.

Under separate cover Dr. Johnson sent me bottles labeled:

> Liq-A-Moni—Gland builder
> 53-D-S—For heart
> Tercapan—For digestion
> 2C+—General builder
> S-G-O—For worms

The bill for the medicines was $28.50.
I never did learn whether Dr. Johnson's saliva tests

involved the use of any gadgets. It is a fact, however, that involvement of the chiropractic field in gadgetry is an old tradition. It began with B. J. Palmer.

One of the beliefs of chiropractic is that subluxations emit heat, like "hot boxes" in the journal bearings of railroad cars. This enables a chiropractor to locate them. In the old days he ran his fingers gently down the patient's back, feeling for warm spots. The process was called "palpating the spine."

It occurred to B. J. Palmer that the process could be profitably automated. In the early 1920's he came out with a wonder-working machine that he called a Neurocalometer. It consisted of a meter with a quivering needle in a polished wooden housing, and a two-pronged electrode that was run up and down the spine. Particularly sharp deflections of the needle indicated warm spots where the subluxations were supposedly located.

Chiropractors clamored for Neurocalometers, but B. J. played his cards close to his chest. They could not be *purchased*, but they could be *leased* for ten-year periods by chiropractors who signed up to take a postgraduate course at the Palmer School. Price of the ten-year lease: $2,200, of which $600 was required as a down payment.

Chiropractors felt that they had no choice. They paid for the lease in whole or in part, and took the PG course.

The chiropractic world was subsequently rocked by the discovery—plain enough to anyone who took two minutes to look at the instrument—that the Neurocalometer was an extremely simple device costing about $30 to put together.* Palmer slashed the leasing price, which only made the original lessees angrier. But wily B. J. easily rode out the storm among his confreres. According to a 1949 New Jersey legislative study, he is reported to have made a cool half-million on the venture.

---

* Much later, in 1960, Stanford Research Institute scientists got hold of a Neurocalometer and found that the "temperature readings" could be drastically changed by simply applying various degrees of pressure to the electrode as it is moved along the spine.

Since the Neurocalometer promotion, many chiropractors seem to have developed an appetite for gadgets that neither modern science nor the requirements of the law have been able to abate. Their passion for these chiropractic devices has kept Food and Drug Administration officials, Post Office Department inspectors, and federal and state law enforcement officials busy for decades, but they have never really been able to catch up.

In 1959 the Federal Food and Drug Administration and the California State Department of Public Health discovered that chiropractors were being sold a "sound therapeutic vibrator," a device that could allegedly cure cancer and other diseases by playing tape recordings of popular music and spoken recitations. The device, called a "Sonus Film-O-Sonic 105," consisted basically of a continuous-tape playback unit of the type used to repeat messages over the telephone. The patient "got the message" in two ways—by listening to the tape with earphones, or by being connected to the machine by two moistened pads and having the vibrations penetrate directly into his body without his hearing them. To cure constipation the machine played a recitation from the Old Testament; to cure cancer, it played "Smoke Gets in Your Eyes."

Illnesses were located and diagnosed by fastening one of the moistened pads to the afflicted person's arm and passing a hand over his body until a "tingling" was felt in the hand or in certain fingers. Heart trouble, for example, was indicated when, with the hand and fingers in a specified position, the finger opposite the patient's left breast "throbbed" while the other fingers did not.

Federal authorities seized a supply of Film-O-Sonics from a Beaumont, Texas, chiropractor who was serving as a dealer. The seizure was contested, so the FDA brought in expert witnesses and prepared for a trial. The day before the trial was to take place, however, the claimant consented to condemnation of the machines. In California, State Public Health officials arrested a San Bernardino chiropractor and a second party, described as the promoters of the same device. It was found that the Film-O-Sonic, which could be made for about $35, was being sold to chiropractors for $500, and California officials estimated that the scheme had brought in $200,000. The pair were convicted and sentenced for violation of state medical practice laws.

In 1962 FDA won a long court fight against one of the most popular of all chiropractic devices, the Ellis Micro-Dynameter, when the U.S. Supreme Court refused to review a lower court action banning it from interstate commerce. The impressive-looking Micro-Dynameter was the centerpiece and the pride of many a chiropractic office; chiropractors even noted in their Yellow Pages phone listings that they offered Micro-Dynameter diagnosis. The machine's circuit—and its value for diagnosing disease—was the same as that of the Drown instruments. It had the same operating elements: two electrodes of dissimilar metal, and a quivering needle. The patient's only function was to complete the circuit. Federal officials tried it on two cadavers; it found them in perfect health.

Chiropractors who used the Micro-Dynameter could buy various vitamin and food supplements to go with it. The administration of these supplements was correlated with the Micro-Dynameter readings and with the location of the alleged subluxations. The subject is discussed in an article, "Electro-Analytical Instruments Used in Chiropractic Practice," by Edwin H. Kimmel, D.C., a member of the faculty of the Chiropractic Institute of New York, which ran in the February and March, 1961, issues of the *Journal of the National Chiropractic Association.**

"Owners of the Micro-Dynameter (MDM)," says the article, "have already received a chart which correlates the meter readings with vitamins ('VIVO-TONE') the patient should be receiving. An example of its application: If the sixth and seventh dorsal are subluxated to

* The American Chiropractic Association was formerly known as the National Chiropractic Association. It changed its name in the early 1960's.

the right, it is recommended that vitamin supplement No. 2 be dispensed. If sixth and seventh dorsal are subluxated to the left, vitamin supplement No. 6 is recommended."

FDA found that more than 5,000 Micro-Dynameters had been sold, most of them to chiropractors, for prices ranging up to $875 each. FDA started rounding up the devices in chiropractic offices and by 1965 about a thousand of them had been located.

Some chiropractors loved and believed in the Micro-Dynameter, and it has died hard. In 1963 I mentioned the federal seizures in an article in the *Saturday Evening Post*. A Phoenix, Arizona, chiropractor wrote a grieving letter to the editor of the *Post*. "Give me the opportunity," he said, "and I will prove beyond a doubt that the Micro-Dynameter is the greatest advance in Physical Diagnosis of the century." At the Parker seminar in 1967 several chiropractors were discussing diagnostic instruments. One of the chiropractors mentioned the Micro-Dynameter wistfully. "It was a good instrument!" he sighed.

(FDA's finding that the Micro-Dynameter cannot tell a dead patient from a live one may have been the reason for a phrase in a leaflet by a chiropractor named H. Robinson, describing an updated version of the Neurocalometer, which the author picked up at the Chiropractic Center of New York in 1964. The instrument, Robinson assures chiropractors, "is no good and is useless on a dead body. It is applicable and practical and CAN BE USED only on a LIVE body.")

In a 1963 court action Roy W. DeWelles, a chiropractor, was sentenced to serve ten years for mail fraud. His assistant, a chiropractor named Richard Broeringmeyer, pleaded guilty and received an eighteen-month sentence. The scheme involved a machine called the Detoxacolon, which, according to the Food and Drug Administration, was nothing more than a pressurized enema device. DeWelles was charged with having claimed that ailments such as cancer, asthma, arthritis, colitis, epilepsy, and high and low blood pressure are caused by toxins in the

65

colon which could be eliminated through irrigation with water and oxygen. This treatment "ignored proven medical facts that point to the dangers of irrigating the colon, including the spreading of infection, possible perforation of the colon walls, and the rinsing out of badly needed salts and other materials required for the colon's proper function," says FDA.

According to FDA, DeWelles and Broeringmeyer traveled around the country selling a package deal to local chiropractors. The Detoxacolon—a wall fixture with dials, glass tubes, rubber hose, and an oxygen tank—would be set up in the chiropractor's office. Thousands of postcards would then be mailed to local residents, offering a free medical examination by a "famous diagnostician." Persons who responded were told that they had serious disorders and were induced to pay up to $500 for a series of Detoxacolon treatments. DeWelles then turned the rest of the job over to the chiropractor in whose office the machine had been installed, receiving from the chiropractor $2,500 for the machine, plus most of the advance payments that the patients had made. At the trial DeWelles admitted receiving over $500,000 for the sale of more than 200 Detoxacolons. Postal inspectors believe that he made at least an additional $1 million through the use of the device himself, while other chiropractors who bought and used the machine took in over $2 million.

In 1965, following an investigation by FDA officials, Frederick I. Sheldon, a Minneapolis, Minnesota, chiropractor, agreed to destroy eleven "Radioclast" devices that he was using. These devices are large consoles whose panels are a veritable forest of dials, lights, switches, and meters. They were manufactured and distributed by L. L. Roby Manufacturing Company and Electronic Instrument Company, both of Tifflin, Ohio. The devices, says FDA, are simply low-voltage generators producing a small electric current. "Scientific" reports on the machines were distributed through International Electronics Research Society, whose address was the same as that of L. L. Roby Manufacturing Company. The gadgets were then unloaded on chiropractors and other credulous fringe practitioners for prices ranging up to $1,200 each. FDA states that thousands were sold.*

Pursuing their path through the chiropractic gadget wilderness, FDA officials visited two chiropractic clinics in Kansas. There they found—and seized—specimens of a gimcrack called "Visual Nerve Tracing Instrument." Promotional literature accompanying the devices, said FDA, made false and misleading claims that it could locate nerve impingement and diagnose such diseases as pulmonary thrombosis, hay fever, chronic bursitis, digestive disturbances, rapid or slow heartbeat, asthma, and diseased viscera. The U.S. District Court in Kansas issued a condemnation decree in 1966.

Meanwhile, some chiropractic groups apparently decided that money could be made in the endorsement business. The Federal Trade Commission charged that a mattress manufacturer had made a deal with twelve state chiropractic associations and the interstate association, of which the state groups are members, whereby, in exchange for the associations' endorsement and promotion of the firm's mattresses, the chiropractors would get a rake-off on each one sold.

FTC stated that, under the terms of the deal, National Mattress Company could claim that its "Posture Queen" mattresses met standards set by the associations, and that they had therapeutic value in spinal conditions. Actually, FTC charged in a complaint against the firm, the mattresses had no therapeutic or health-giving properties and were "not designed in accordance with specific en-

---

* In recent years some chiropractic groups have cooperated with federal and state authorities in attempting to relieve chiropractors of some of the more absurd devices of which many of them have been enamored. Following the Supreme Court's decision upholding the banning of the Micro-Dynameter, state chiropractic associations have cooperated in rounding up the devices from chiropractor's offices. In the Sheldon case, the Minnesota State Board of Chiropractic Examiners held the hearings that resulted in destruction of the devices.

gineering standards established by a chiropractic association." In fact, said FTC, the alleged standards are "nonexistent." The case was settled in July, 1967, by a consent order in which the firm agreed to give up the health claims and drop the deal with the chiropractors.*

FDA's weary roundup of gadgets continues. In February, 1968, it reported seizure of a "Chiroscope Electronic Detector," the labeling of which, said FDA, "lacked adequate directions for use for analysis and diagnosis" of certain conditions of the spine. Adequate directions, FDA added, "could not be written, since the device was worthless for its intended purposes." A default decree was issued and the contraption was turned over to FDA.

The use of such devices by chiropractors causes one to want to know more about the schooling that a chiropractor receives.

---

* Federal Trade Commission consent orders are issued for the purpose of settling cases and eliminating the activity of which the commission has complained, without resorting to further litigation. They do not constitute an admission by parties involved that they have violated the law.

CHAPTER SIX

Schooldays

"SINCE I'VE BEEN DRIVING A TRUCK FOR TWELVE YEARS WITH no chance of doing much better, my uncle promised to pay my way to your college if I would do it. I wasn't too good of a student in high school, but I like to read a lot, and I read a little about chiropractic, and it really seems to be the coming thing."

The above is an excerpt from a letter written to one of the nation's leading chiropractic colleges by a person seeking admission. The college replied asking for a letter of recommendation and a transcript of high school credits, and enclosing two examinations for the prospective student to take. It received the examinations back from the student; they showed a tenth-grade level of achievement. The letter of recommendation, from a person in a trucking company, said, "Although I find him quite dependable, in all honesty I cannot say that he utilizes a great deal of imagination in his work. However, this lack of imagination should not be taken as a rebuke, but merely as an evaluation of his qualities."

From the prospective student himself the college received an eloquent letter explaining why he was unable to provide a copy of his high school transcript.

> I went downtown to the main offices of the Board of education, and boy did I get the run-around. I never saw so much red tape in ally my life. But after much running around and being battered from piller to post, I finally got to see the guy who is suppose to be in charge of high school credits. After he took a lot of time looking all over the place for my credits, he finally said that he was sorry, but somehow my records got misplaced, and he just didn't know what to do now, because I guess they lost all my records. I hope this don't interfere with my being accepted.

The college wrote a letter to the Board of Education in the applicant's city, and received a reply stating that it had no record of such a person ever having graduated from the city's schools. The college then wrote to the applicant suggesting that he take a GED (General Educational Development) test. The applicant replied asking for conditional acceptance. The college replied in the affirmative; the applicant was enrolled in the fall class. (He subsequently received a letter from a female student at the college who was to be his "big sister," inviting him to see her if he needed any help; she signed it "Chiropractically yours.")

Actually, the prospective student did not exist—and neither did the trucking company that wrote his letter of recommendation, for that matter. The letter was one of seven different semiliterate letters written to seven of the nation's best-known colleges of chiropractic, in which the applicant sought admission but could not produce a high school diploma. Five of the schools accepted and enrolled the applicant.

Another of the letters was supposedly from a single girl in her thirties named Bonnie, who had been running a massage parlor in Chicago for five years. "We work on both men and women and do pretty good," she wrote to one of the schools. "I never went to high school." The college to which it was addressed sent her an application. Bonnie filled it out, listing a nonexistent grade school and affirming that she had had no high school. The college replied, suggesting that she take a GED test. "Is it really necessary for me to take a bunch of tests to get into your school?" Bonnie replied. "I am sure that i would make a good chiropractor and I bet that I could do just as good in school as some of these young kids who went to highschool." The college replied, offering her conditional acceptance and permitting her to take the GED sometime during her first year. Bonnie wrote back that that would be fine, "As I am going to be very busy in trying to wind up all my affairs here in Chicago. before coming to _____, I don't think that I'M going to get a chance to take these GED tests here in Chciago,"

A third letter was from an applicant who had been in the army but had not received an honorable discharge. "I have just been generally discharged from the Army after serving 10 years in the Army Medical Corp.," the applicant wrote. "While I was in the Army I got real interested in helping sickpeople become well again. But since I am not a highschool graduate I won't be able to go to medical school. Besides, some of thoise medical doctorss are real butchers anyway." The college granted him conditional acceptance.

As we have already seen in the chapter describing the origins of chiropractic, the schooling of chiropractors in the early days was brief, and there were no admission requirements to the schools other than the ability to pay for the course. Nowadays chiropractic colleges offer four-year courses. Based on available information, however, their admission standards appear to remain low, their faculties offer limited commonly recognized academic credentials, their equipment and facilities are meager, and their students have little if any opportunity either for research or for clinical work in hospitals.

According to the HEW Report, there are twelve schools

71

of chiropractic in the United States. None of them is accredited by any recognized educational accrediting body. The American Chiropractic Association (mixers) recognizes eight of them and the International Chiropractors Association (straights) recognizes three.* Each association has set up an accrediting body of its own, which has accredited the colleges that its association recognizes. These two accrediting groups do not enjoy recognition by the U.S. Office of Education or the recognized academic accrediting bodies.**

The educational purpose of chiropractic colleges has to a great extent been molded by state chiropractic licensing acts passed by most states. The most important provision in the licensing laws is that aspiring chiropractors must pass a series of "basic science examinations" in anatomy, bacteriology, chemistry, diagnosis, hygiene, pathology, physiology, and public health. The same requirement is made of aspiring medical doctors.

These requirements were enacted with good intention, but their actual impact has hardly been beneficial. The passage of such written examinations does not qualify one to treat the sick. As a matter of practice, medical students take and pass the exams at an early stage of their medical education, and spend years of additional study, internship, and research before they are licensed to practice. By contrast, almost the entire thrust of chiropractic

---

* A list of the colleges and the associations that recognize them is contained in Appendix B.

** The three recognized educational bodies that accredit institutions of higher education in the United States are the Federation of Regional Accrediting Commissions of Higher Education, the National Commission on Accrediting, and the Office of Education of the Federal Government. The Federation of Regional Accrediting Commissions of Higher Education accredits colleges and universities through its member regional associations. The National Commission on Accrediting and the Office of Education list approved accrediting agencies for the professions. Chiropractic schools are not recognized or listed by any of these accrediting organizations.

education is aimed at getting the students past these examinations, which constitute the principal hurdle they must surmount to enter their profession.

In five states the same basic science exams are given to students of chiropractic and students of medicine, and the exams are graded by the same board on a uniform standard. A set of statistics covering a period of several years in these states showed that an average of 81.4 percent of all medical students passed the exams on their first try. An average of 84.5 percent of chiropractic students failed.

Chiropractors are exerting strenuous efforts to prevent such information from being compiled. The American Chiropractic Association is pushing to prohibit exam applicants from having to list the college from which they are applying; this would make it difficult to tell how chiropractic students as a group fared on the exams. The International Chiropractors Association is working to prevent medical and chiropractic students from having their exams graded by the same board. The value to chiropractors of the latter procedure has been well demonstrated. In states in which medical students' exams are graded by a board of M.D.'s, and chiropractic students' exams are graded by a board of chiropractors, the showing of the chiropractic students improves tremendously.

In chiropractic colleges it is common lore among the students that some states have "easy" exam standards and other states are "tough." Some students establish residency in "easy" states in order to take the exams there; they can then achieve licensure through reciprocity in other states where reciprocal licensing arrangements have been established. Thus, for example, a Palmer student from Tennessee told a reporter that he planned to take his basic science exams in Alabama and then obtain reciprocity in Tennessee, because Alabama's examinations were known to be easier.

The relatively poor performance of chiropractic students in these examinations reflects not only the colleges' low admission standards but the educational backgrounds of their instructors.

The September 19, 1966 issue of the *Journal of the American Medical Association* (*JAMA*) carried a report entitled "Educational Background of Chiropractic School Faculties." The report was based on a review of the catalogues of eleven U.S. chiropractic colleges, plus one in Canada, and a check of the academic backgrounds of the listed faculty members.

The *JAMA* report says that, in contrast to the procedure of accredited colleges and universities, three of the twelve catalogs do not list the school's faculties. Three others that list the faculty members and their degrees neglect to indicate what institutions granted the degrees—again in contrast to the practice of accredited institutions. It was thus possible to check the academic credentials of the faculties of only seven of the colleges.

Most members of the faculties of these colleges are listed as holding the degree of D.C.—Doctor of Chiropractic. This, as we have seen, is not an accredited or recognized academic degree.

Turning to actual recognized degrees from accredited institutions that are held by faculty members of the seven chiropractic colleges, *JAMA*'s report states that less than 50 percent list even bachelor's degrees from accredited colleges or universities. In the public school system of most states today a bachelor's degree is required even to teach kindergarten. Where academic degrees are listed, they are often in subjects bearing little or no relationship to the subjects the faculty members are teaching.

In some cases the faculty members list degrees that have no recognized status in the academic community. According to the *JAMA* report, other faculty members list degrees that must politely be called "unconfirmed." In some of these instances no record can be found that the listed college ever existed. In others, the college exists, but it stated, when queried, that it has no record that the faculty member ever went there. Again, in some instances, the colleges stated that the person in question attended but never graduated.

With 1,100 students, the Palmer College of Chiropractic remains the largest of the chiropractic colleges from the standpoint of enrollment. Its 1965–1966 catalog lists twenty-nine faculty members, of whom only eight list recognized four-year degrees, and only three list any recognized degree beyond the bachelor's degree.

The dean of the faculty, the chairman of the X-ray department, and the director of education and professor of anatomy, all holding the rank of full professor, do not list a single recognized academic degree among them, even at the bachelor's level.

The person designated as dean of basic sciences and professor of anatomy and diagnosis lists no recognized four-year degree. Neither do an assistant professor of chemistry and bacteriology, an assistant professor of anatomy and pathology, or the two instructors in X ray. Among the faculty members who do have degrees, an associate professor of physiology and pathology has a bachelor's degree in animal husbandry. An associate professor of chemistry and diagnosis has a B.S. degree in business administration. He is also director of athletics.

Two schools with larger faculties are the Los Angeles College of Chiropractic, listing forty-four faculty members in its 1964–1965 catalog, and the Chiropractic Institute of New York, listing thirty-one members in its 1965–1966 catalog.

The president of the Los Angeles College of Chiropractic lists a Ph.D. degree, but does not indicate where it came from. The administrative dean, the dean of instruction, the dean of the graduate school, the dean of students, the director of research, the director of clinics, and the dean emeritus do not list a bachelor's degree among them.

The chairman of the anatomy department, who lists himself as a "certified pathologist," holds a bachelor's

75

degree in education. The acting chairman and sole member of the department of obstetrics and gynecology lists no recognized academic degree.

On the "clinic staff," the heads of the departments of roentgenology, EENT, cardiology, neurology, and orthopedics list no academic degrees. One member of the department of chemistry and nutrition actually does list no less than three recognized academic degrees—a B.S. in electrical engineering, an M.A. in education, and an O.D. in optometry.

Another faculty member lists a "D.P.M." degree from the "Los Angeles College of Drugless Physicians." It is not known what the letters stand for. Another member lists an "O.C.R." degree. The letters apparently stand for "Order of Christ the King."

The 1965–1966 bulletin of the Chiropractic Institute of New York (the school of which Clarence W. Weiant is dean emeritus) lists the faculty but does not say who teaches what. The president and vice-president of the school list no academic degrees.

The faculty listings of the various colleges are often followed by unrecognized or meaningless academic initials. The president of one chiropractic college lists himself as an "N.D."—doctor of naturopathy—without indicating what institution granted the degree. The N.D. degree from any institution is unrecognized by modern science.

In at least some instances, the overall facilities of chiropractic schools have been as inferior as the educational backgrounds of their faculties. In 1960, Stanford Research Institute, under a grant from the John Randolph Haynes and Dora Haynes Foundation, prepared and published a study of the programs and facilities of three chiropractic colleges in California—the Los Angeles College of Chiropractic, the Cleveland College of Chiropractic, and the Hollywood College of Chiropractic. The Hollywood College of Chiropractic refused to cooperate with Stanford Institute in the project, and would not permit institute teams to visit its facilities.* Institute teams made a number of visits to the other two schools during a six-month period in 1958–1959, and compiled statistical and other information on all three colleges.

The study of the faculties of the two cooperating colleges produced a familiar story. Of twenty-nine faculty members, only ten claimed to have bachelor's degrees, and in four of these cases the college from which the faculty member claimed to have a degree denied that such a degree had been granted.

The rest of the institute's study presents a rare inside look at the type of program and curriculum that has turned out many of today's D.C.'s. "In their curricula, chiropractic schools use course titles and textbooks similar to those used in medical and osteopathic schools," the institute's report says. "However, their teaching approach is centered almost entirely on classroom lectures and practical work in out-patient clinics. No hospital in-patient training is available.

"Although a number of laboratory courses are listed in school catalogs," the report continues, "there was no evidence that the chemistry laboratories were in use at any time during the Institute project team visits. . . . Similarly, the libraries were found to be seldom used. . . . The laboratories were not equipped and the libraries not staffed to serve the purposes for which they were intended. These conditions suggest that libraries and laboratories do not play an important part in the education of a chiropractor."

Total fixed assets of the Los Angeles College, including the three two-story brick buildings in which the college was housed, were valued at $186,069. "However," says the report, "during the course of many visits by Institute

---

* This college, originally called the Pasadena College of Chiropractic, became the Drown College of Chiropractic (see Chapter Five) in 1948. In 1949 its name was again changed, to Hollywood College of Chiropractic. It was later absorbed into the Los Angeles College of Chiropractic.

personnel in the period June, 1958, to February, 1959, the chemistry laboratory was found to contain no more in the way of equipment than chemistry benches. No reagent bottles or chemicals were in view, and the laboratory was odorless. The benches, which were newly painted in the summer of 1958, were free of the chemical stains and bottle marks commonly seen in a laboratory which is used. . . . The chemical stockroom was also odorless; it contained several prepared solutions, stored in dusty cartons, and a five-gallon tin of acetone and isopropyl alcohol."

The school's library contained about four thousand books, and the periodical racks carried about forty magazines and journals. There was seating capacity for exactly four students. The library was often closed during the hours that it was scheduled to be open; there was dust on the tabletops. "In general," says the report, "the library facilities are meager and appear to be seldom used."

At the Cleveland college, a smaller school, all activities, says the report, "are carried on in two single-family dwellings which have been made over to fit the needs of the college." The college estimated the value of its properties at $75,000 to $80,000, and its equipment at $15,000 to $20,000.

"The CCC [Cleveland College of Chiropractic] buildings contain four lecture rooms, the largest of which has a capacity of about fifty students," the report states. "The other lecture rooms hold no more than about thirty students each. Laboratory space in the college has been converted from the kitchen and dining room areas of one of the residences."

The laboratory facilities were so meager, the Stanford teams found, that the college could not even offer lab work to compare with that given in the public schools.

Equipment observed in the laboratory by Institute personnel during visits to the college included about twelve test tubes, one or two flasks, and a variety of dusty bottles, all stored in a small room adjoining the laboratory. . . . There were no chemicals stored on the grounds and no odor of chemicals in the laboratory, the laboratory storeroom, or elsewhere on CCC property. Storage space under the work benches was empty except for a few discarded cartons, a roll of paper towels, and several similar items. In view of the quantity and type of equipment in evidence, laboratory use would necessarily be limited to only the most rudimentary experiments.

The library was also rudimentary; it was housed in a single room seven feet three inches wide and twelve feet eight inches long. "There are between 1,500 and 2,000 volumes in the stacks. Seating space for reading is provided in a classroom located next to the library rather than in the library itself." Less than 1 percent of the books in the library, the researchers found, had been written in the last ten years, and there were no periodicals. When a member of the school's staff was asked about the antiquity of the library's holdings, the staff member replied that "things are happening so fast in chiropractic that it would cost too much to buy new books all the time."

Conditions in the California colleges, and in other chiropractic colleges, may have improved in some respects since 1960. However, the general picture of chiropractic education remains seriously inadequate. Its shortcomings, says the HEW Report, "raise serious doubts as to the qualifications of chiropractors generally to make an adequate diagnosis and effectively treat patients."

In their classroom work, chiropractic students use both standard medical works and texts written by chiropractors. One wonders how the students—or the professors—reconcile the two kinds of information that they find in these two types of books.

According to HEW's 1968 Report, the most commonly used chiropractic textbook is *The Neurodynamics of the Vertebral Subluxation,* by A. E. Homewood, D.C., N.D. (n.p.: published by the author, 1962). Homewood is described in the Report as dean emeritus of the Canadian Memorial Chiropractic College and a member of the American Chiropractic Association's Commission on Standardization of Chiropractic Principles. The Report quotes Homewood's book as saying,

> While it is not the purpose of the writer to derogate practitioners of other forms of healing, it is of the utmost concern to awaken an appreciation in the minds of doctors of chiropractic for the heritage left by D. D. Palmer, which provides the basis for the most complete understanding of the patient as a unit of structure and function yet to be devised by man to this date.

On the relationship of chiropractic treatment to heart attacks, the Report gives the following quotation from the book:

> Experience has established the fact that the administration of chiropractic adjusting is efficacious in handling both the acute and chronic cases of coronary occlusion, but no button has been located, either theoretically or clinically, that may be pushed in every patient to make the correction.

On the germ theory of disease, the Report quotes Homewood's book as saying,

> The doctor of chiropractic is well aware of the presence of bacteria and concedes that these minute organisms play a role in many diseases. He would, however, emphatically deny that micro-organisms are THE cause of the diseases with which they are associated. . . .*

The second most widely used chiropractic text, says HEW's Report, is *Chiropractic Principles and Technic*

---

* HEW Report, pp. 153, 154, 160, 167, 174.

for Use by Students and Practitioners, by Joseph Janse, D.C., R. H. Houser, D.C., and B. F. Wells, D.O., D.C., copyright 1947 by the National College of Chiropractic. Among the authors, the most distinguished appears to be Joseph Janse. He is president of the National College of Chiropractic, a leading "mixer" school, and has recently (1966) been chairman of both the Committee on Public Health and the Committee on Chiropractic Standardization of the American Chiropractic Association.

As a basic text on a medical subject, *Chiropractic Principles* is perhaps unique. The 660-page work contains no bibliography, no bibliographic references, and not a single footnote. In the entire text I was able to find only two references to other medical works, each one sentence long. In neither instance is the publisher, date, or page number of the reference cited.

The only medical person whose opinion on any subject is cited at length is a Dr. Alfred Walton, whose three-paragraph endorsement of chiropractic appears in the text. Dr. Walton was one of a small group of M.D.'s who became converts to chiropractic, and who actually became chiropractors, during the infancy of the cult.* He published a monograph endorsing chiropractic ideas in 1908, and died in 1920.

"Vertebral subluxations," readers of *Chiropractic Principles* are told, "are the cause of the production and continuance of disease. . . . Probably in all abnormal states there is a demonstrable spinal lesion."

Many maladies are discussed. Some examples are:

The tenth dorsal vertebra is found subluxated in all cases of kidney diseases.

* * *

The second lumbar vertebra virtually always is found subluxated in constipation, showing the re-

---

* For further information on these M.D.-chiropractors, see Chapter Ten. A testimonial by Dr. Walton is among those used in the Parker Chiropractic Research Foundation's leaflet "M.D.'s Comment on Chiropractic," discussed in that chapter.

lationship between its frequency and this exceedingly common disorder.

• • •

A subluxation in the upper cervical and upper dorsal regions will interfere with the action of the heart.

• • •

A subluxation involving the fourth dorsal vertebra will result in various disorders of the liver.

The authors concede that germs have something to do with human disease. But this need not worry the chiropractor. Germs can do their dirty work only when the body has been weakened by subluxations. When the subluxations are adjusted, the germs fold up their tents and steal away. The book cites typhoid fever as an illustration. The direct cause of the disease, it says, is the typhoid bacillus.

> This bacillus is not, however, the primary cause: for by this cause one must understand that state or condition of certain parts which makes the action of the typhoid bacillus possible. This primary cause is subluxation of vertebrae, which by producing a disturbed nerve supply, and thereby diminishing the resistance of those parts for which the typhoid bacillus has a selective action, make possible their activity in those parts. Therefore the subluxations are the primary, indirect and predisposing cause of typhoid fever, and the typhoid bacillus is the secondary, exciting and direct cause.

Faced even with foes such as the typhoid bacillus, the chiropractor, therefore, can simply adjust the sufferer's spine. "It is found that the fever subsides rapidly when these subluxations are corrected," the text says. The same principle, it adds, applies "'to all infectious and contagious diseases.'"

Immunization is strongly opposed by many leaders of chiropractic, and is condemned in a number of chiropractic texts. One of the enemies of immunization is C. W. Weiant, dean emeritus of the Chiropractic Institute of New York. His book *Rational Bacteriology*, written with R. J. Watkins and J. R. Verner,* is used as a text in many chiropractic colleges. "Diphtheria antitoxin and toxoid," says this book, "are both not only worthless in practically every case, but also virulent and injurious in all cases." Rabies serum is "utterly worthless." Typhoid vaccine has been "completely exposed" as "worthless." In cases of tetanus, "there is not the slightest excuse for the toxin-antitoxin." By contrast, "drugless healers have been highly successful in handling diphtheria without serums," and diseases such as gonorrhea and cerebrospinal meningitis "respond readily to non-medical methods."

In 1965 chiropractic educators and textbook writers had an opportunity to air their beliefs at a trial in Louisiana. Louisiana is one of two states in the Union (the other is Mississippi) that have resisted the pressures of the chiropractic lobby, and refuse to license chiropractors or to legalize their practice. A chiropractor named Jerry R. England, on behalf of himself and a number of other chiropractors, brought an unsuccessful suit against the Louisiana Board of Medical Examiners, to try to force the board to permit them to practice chiropractic in the state. In the trial, a number of luminaries of the chiropractic world journeyed to Louisiana to testify.

One was Joseph Janse. Here are excerpts from his testimony under cross-examination:

Q: What specific centers would you adjust for tetanus?
A: To normalize the vasomotor extension, of course, you would adjust in the lower lumbar spine.

. . .

Q: What is the chiropractic treatment for polio?
A: Chiropractic treatment for polio in the initial

---

* Verner is the author of a work called *Vaccination: A Fraud.*

stages of polio, in the prodroma, is the adjustment primarily.

. . .

Q (by the Court): What would you do with a patient while you are making up your mind as to whether he has meningitis?

A: I would, in this patient—I would give this patient a careful chiropractic adjustment.

Another witness was William D. Harper, former dean and now president of the Texas Chiropractic College, a member of the American Chiropractic Association's Commission on Standardization of Chiropractic Principles, and also the author of a book on chiropractic entitled *Anything Can Cause Anything* (San Antonio, Texas: published by the author, 1964):

Q: In your book, Dr. Harper, I get the impression from reading it that at one point you say that some workings of the individual psychic thought could cause a subluxation?

A: Yes, because psychic irritation of the nervous system can through irritation of the cord and into the anterior horn cause muscle contraction and in turn produce a subluxation in which case the subluxation becomes one of the symptoms of the complex and not the cause of the phenomena as long as the original irritation, be it clinical or psychic, remains.

. . .

Q: In other words, I could think myself into a subluxation?

A: You could. Now, pardon me, may I say one thing. That is one of the, as a perfect example, I have suffered today from the irritation of being up on this stand. This is my first experience. I am demonstrating the fact today.

. . .

Q: You mean you think I am giving you a sub-luxation?

A: Yes.

. . .

Q: Could you tell us what vertebra is affected by cross-examination?

A: All of them.

Q: So that the gamut of diseases is possible as a result of being a witness?

A: Chronic irritation of the nervous system.

Q: You could get polio?

A: It's possible.

Perhaps one reason that chiropractic students find such teachers and teachings acceptable is that they are completely insulated from an experience that is a central part of the education of medical students. No hospital accredited by the Joint Commission on Hospital Accreditation permits chiropractors or chiropractic students to make use of its facilities either for seeing patients or for intern training.* The chiropractic student, therefore, graduates, becomes a "doctor," and treats human illness without ever having had any experience with hospitalized patients.

For chiropractic students, however, there is at least one consolation. They get better grades than students in medical school. The Stanford Institute found that, of all grades awarded by Cleveland Chiropractic College to its students during a five-month period in 1958, 60 percent were As. Of the rest, 30 percent were Bs, 6 percent were Cs, 3 percent were Ds, and 1 percent were Fs. Of all

---

* The laws of all states except North Carolina also prohibit chiropractors from having access to hospitals. North Carolina's law, dating back to 1919, permits chiropractors access to hospitals. The state's health officials, however, were surprised to learn of this provision of the law when it was called to their attention in 1967, and no official could recall any instance in which the right had been exercised.

grades granted by the Los Angeles College over several comparable periods, 78 percent were As and Bs.

And, as for hospital facilities, if they have none in their training, they can at least refer their more serious cases to Spears Chiropractic Sanitarium and Hospital in Denver, Colorado, after they begin their practice.

It is to this unique institution that we must next turn our attention.

CHAPTER SEVEN

The House That Leo Built

"PAIN OF ARTHRITIS CONQUERED BY NEW DISCOVERIES! Research at Spears Chiropractic Hospital has opened the door to health for thousands of sufferers who have been led to believe there was no relief."

"MULTIPLE SCLEROSIS? Research at Spears Hospital has further added to the effectiveness of Chiropractic's attack on this crippler."

"CEREBRAL PALSY? SPEARS researchers have developed corrective methods for the treatment of cerebral palsy, mental deficiency, epilepsy and kindred afflictions of children."

These are excerpts from newspaper ads for Spears Chiropractic Sanitarium and Hospital published between 1964 and 1966. Even claims of this kind were not on my mind, however, as I walked up the path to the hospital's main entrance in Denver. I was thinking of the documents I had been poring over just an hour before at the Denver Better Business Bureau. They showed that a number of persons whose testimonials had been published by Spears as having been helped or cured were actually dead. Some had died before their testimonials were published.

Inside the attractive lobby I told the receptionist that I had some personal medical problems and wished to make an appointment for a physical exam. I actually did not intend to take an exam, but was seeking only an opportunity to see the hospital without arousing suspicion. We made an appointment for me to come in the next morning, and I then asked if someone could show me around today while I was there. "Of course," the receptionist said.

In a few moments a lady came to the lobby, identifying herself as a member of the hospital's public relations staff. She was a short, energetic woman who said she was once a newspaper reporter. As we toured the building she told me an extended tale of how chiropractic had cured her of her ailments.

First we paused to look at a portrait hanging in the lobby. "That's D. D. Palmer," she said reverently. "He's the great doctor who discovered the chiropractic method of healing." In this portrait, I noted, he looked even glummer than usual.

We then crossed the lobby and stopped in front of a silver metallic bust of a beaming, bald, cherub-like man with the initials LS in fancy script on his necktie. "That," she said, "is Dr. Leo Spears himself—the man who healed so many people, and who founded this hospital. I knew him when he was alive."

"He must have been quite a man," I said.

"Oh, he was!" she exclaimed.

The lady then took me through two floors of patients' rooms, solariums, wards, and treatment rooms. I saw many patients—perhaps as many as seventy-five.

"What diseases do they have?" I asked after we had left a room full of crippled men.

"Well, it varies," she replied. "At the moment about 40 percent of the patients have muscular dystrophy or multiple sclerosis."

When we went back downstairs the lady said, "I'm

sorry that we can't go up to the children's floor. It's lunch hour and they can't be disturbed."

"What types of disease do most of them have?"

"Many are cerebral palsy patients. We have a special program here at Spears for cerebral palsy. We believe that it is caused by a misshapen skull that pinches the brain. Our treatment consists of remolding the shape of the children's heads. It has to be done while the skulls are still soft. I know that you'd be fascinated and I'm sorry that we can't go up."

Other treatments offered at Spears, I found, included colonic irrigation ("Colonic irrigation is a hangover of a theory of 'auto-intoxication' that was popular fifty years ago," says the Arthritis Foundation. "It was discarded years ago."), "special diets," "scientific fasting," and a treatment called "nerve and cell goading," which "enables us to relieve most types of pain and force nature to speed up her healing."

At the basis of Spears treatment chiropractic reigns supreme. My guide and I entered a treatment room containing two adjustment tables, each with several sets of independently adjustable red cushions. "This," she said, placing her fingers gently on one of them, "is the heart of the chiropractic treatment of disease. It is the chiropractic adjustment table. All other treatments are strictly an adjunct to this. The true cure of human illness is chiropractic adjustment of the spine."

As we left she gave me a large packet of literature—booklets, flyers, and a hospital newspaper called the *Spears Sanigram,* all filled with testimonials of patients allegedly helped or cured. Three of the booklets dealt, respectively, with arthritis, multiple sclerosis, and cerebral palsy, the three diseases featured in the Spears newspaper ads cited at the beginning of this chapter.

The booklet on arthritis says that "long years of research at Spears on thousands of patients have shown the following to be among the 'usual causes':

"Pressure on nerves and blood vessels by slightly displaced or misaligned bones of the spine—and possibly the bones of the other joints also.

"Excessive, or diminished, activity of hormone-producing glands.

"Toxins from frequent or long-standing infections.

"Improper metabolism when foods are not properly burned, or oxidized; and sometimes from excessive ingestion of improper food combinations."

Dr. William S. Clark, president of the Arthritis Foundation, says, "We have absolutely no evidence that any of these factors is involved in the cause of any of the forms of crippling arthritis."

The booklet on multiple sclerosis states:

Our experience with thousands of cases at Spears Hospital indicates that the basic cause of multiple sclerosis is usually an injury to the spine and spinal cord, which results in cord and nerve pressures and impingements. These pressures interrupt the flow of nerve energy and of nutritional elements to the muscles. Robbed of their normal nutrition and nerve supply, the legs and arms weaken, become unresponsive and often are subject to muscle spasms.

Dr. James Q. Simmons, Jr., director of medical programs for the National Multiple Sclerosis Society, says:

The scientific evidence available to us does not support this statement by Spears. Unfortunately, the cause and cure of multiple sclerosis are both unknown. The disease is often characterized by remissions, so that, in any group of patients under observation, 50 percent or more appear to improve. This makes multiple sclerosis a fruitful field for unproven theories and treatments. We receive letters at the Society from victims of the disease and their families who are prepared to pay over their savings and even mortgage their homes, to make the journey to Spears for treatment. However, we have no indication that Spears has knowledge of the disease that is unknown to medical research. Neither has Spears demonstrated to the scientific community that it has methods of treatment superior to, or unknown to, persons working in established channels of therapy and rehabilitation.

The booklet on cerebral palsy confirmed what my guide at Spears had told me about the hospital's theory and treatment. The most frequent cause of cerebral palsy, the booklet said, is "a flattened or otherwise distorted skull, creating pressure on the brain."

For many years it [was] believed that cerebral palsy resulted from brain *injury. Something* happened to the brain that prevented its normal functioning. However, it was not until Spears researchers launched an intensive study of *skull patterns* that the real or prevailing causative factor was revealed. They found that the bony structure of abnormally shaped skulls pressed against tender and highly sensitive brain tissues.

The treatment was called Spears Skull Remoulding. "The one way to rid the brain of pressure is to correct the cause. The only way to eliminate the cause, when skull distortion is a factor, is to remould the skull to its normal shape."

Children should be put into treatment as early as possible, the booklet says, since skulls are easiest to mold when the patient is very young. "If not too severe, maximum correction of the cause can frequently be made in two to six months when the patient is less than one year old; in three to twelve months up to the age of three; six to eighteen months of intensive treatment for those of five years or less. Excellent results have been obtained in many cases five to seven years old; and some good results are even possible at more advanced ages."

Dr. Brewster S. Miller, director of research for the United Cerebral Palsy Research and Educational Foundation, says:

> I know of no scientific evidence from any source which gives validity to the claim of the Spears Chiropractic Hospital that "cerebral palsy is caused by a flat or otherwise distorted skull, creating pressure on the brain." I must say that the Spears system of reshaping or remolding distorted skulls in babies is frightening to contemplate.

Another Spears pamphlet available in the early 1960's was on cancer. It consisted of a question-and-answer interview with the late Dr. Leo Spears himself. Cancer, said Dr. Spears, is caused by "interference with nerve supply to the area affected," and "body wastes—poisons—resulting from poor elimination from one or more of the eliminative organs." The cure included "spinal adjustments, which relieve nerve pressures and re-establish control of nerve energy."

Dr. Roald Grant, vice-president for Professional Education of the American Cancer Society and co-author of the society's publication *Unproven Methods of Cancer Treatment*, says, "There is absolutely no scientifically valid evidence that 'interference with nerve supply' or 'poor elimination from one or more of the eliminative organs' causes cancer, or that spinal column manipulation or 'adjustments' to 'relieve nerve pressures and re-establish control of nerve energy' has any beneficial effect in the treatment of cancer."

Dr. Leo Spears was a 1921 graduate of the Palmer School. His chiropractor's license was revoked in 1924 for "dishonorable, immoral and unprofessional practice" but was later restored. In 1943 he began construction of the Spears Chiropractic Sanitarium and Hospital. Under his leadership it mushroomed into a multimillion-dollar operation that has treated over 100,000 patients and has become the Mecca of chiropractic. Dr. Spears became the personal chiropractor of U.S. Senator William Langer and rose to national prominence. Chiropractors from all over the country refer their patients to Spears, and the Parker Chiropractic Research Foundation suggests that they hang a framed picture of the hospital in their reception rooms.

Dr. Leo made his big name on cancer. Spears literature on the subject blanketed the country. One booklet said on its cover, "CHIROPRACTIC ANSWER TO CANCER . . . SENSATIONAL GUARANTEE . . . *Cancer Relief or Money Back!*" Inside, the booklet said, "Happy results on thousands of cancer patients treated at the Spears Chiropractic Sanitarium and Hospital indicate that our researchers have found the major causes of cancer." Cancer patients beat a path to the hospital's door, and the hospital published reams of testimonials of those who had been supposedly helped or cured.

In April, 1954, the federal government seized three devices called Neuromicrometers from Spears Hospital, charging that they were misbranded. Dr. Leo was belligerent. "If you take these machines," he told the U.S. marshal making the seizure, "there's going to be trouble." Spears Hospital, he said, had found the causes of cancer, and "will continue to do our work here despite outrages such as this." When the court hearing came, however, Spears was more compliant, and consented to a decree by which the machines were condemned.

Dr. Leo was often in court suing people. In 1943 a Denver doctor wrote on the death certificate of a Spears patient that she had died as a result of neglect at Spears Hospital. Dr. Leo sued the doctor for $300,000, but lost.

In 1951 he was cited in an article called "Cancer Quacks" in *Collier's* magazine. He sued *Collier's* for $24 million. During the trial he admitted that five out of six persons giving testimonials in a Spears cancer pamphlet were actually dead. It also came out that Dr. Leo did not recognize a malignancy in a child that was brought to the hospital; she was treated for rheumatism. He lost the case.

In 1954 he filed an $11-million action against the Denver Better Business Bureau, the Denver *Post*, the Colorado State Medical Society, and more than eighty other parties, alleging that they had been conspiring to damage his business.

In the ensuing court action, Denver *Post* reporter Robert M. Byers testified that, in working on a story on Spears' alleged discovery of an effective method for treating cancer, he had been given the records of eighty-three Spears cancer patients by Dr. Spears. Checking them out one by one, he found that sixty were known or strongly believed to be dead, and, of the twenty-three known to be alive, eighteen had been diagnosed as having cancer only by Spears Hospital, and none of the diagnoses was based on a medical biopsy.

On the witness stand, Dr. Spears was asked if he claimed that diabetes could be cured by a chiropractor. "We've had a good many cases in which the person so treated didn't have to take insulin," he replied. The defense attorney asked him if it were not true that he himself was a diabetic, and was taking insulin on the prescription of a medical doctor. Spears confessed that it was so.

He lost the case.

Spears wrote a number of books, including a novel called *Hellcrest* which was published in Denver in 1929, and a book called *Sex Problems Solved*. But his most substantial work was a book called *Spears Painless System of Chiropractic* (fifth edition, copyright 1950), which is still sold to chiropractors for $24 and to chiropractic students for $12. (In his deposition in the Denver Better Business Bureau–Denver *Post* libel action, Spears testified that the first thousand copies were sold for $100 each, after which the lower price was established. According to Spears records, the books cost $1.65 each to produce.) The book sets forth "unusually effective methods of treating and relieving such 'incurable' diseases as arthritis, epilepsy, multiple sclerosis, infantile paralysis, diabetes mellitus,* cancer, rheumatic fever, heart ailments, etc." It also describes his "discovery" that "infantile skull distortion, causing bony pressure upon the brain, is responsible for most cases of cerebral palsy and mental deficiency."

The book recommends that, the more desperately ill and weak the patient is, the more often he should be adjusted. ". . . when a patient is critically ill," says the text, "instead of lengthening the period between adjustments because he appears weak, it is most usually necessary to increase the number of adjustments in proportion to his weakness. . . . Lockjaw, peritonitis, acute appendicitis, gallstone attacks, advanced pneumonia, advanced diphtheria, advanced scarlet fever, advanced typhoid and the like require close attention and adjustments sometimes as often as fifteen minutes to two hours apart."**

In May, 1956, Dr. Leo Spears passed on to whatever his reward might be, and the hospital was taken over by his two nephews, Howard and Dan, both chiropractors. Under their regime the hospital continued to offer treatment for almost every human condition. "Spears Hospital," says a booklet, "is equipped and staffed to handle practically every type of case and every known disease, including those problem cases that need specialized study and care; and cases with such stubborn conditions as cancer, multiple sclerosis, cerebral palsy, mental deficiency, polio, epilepsy, rheumatic fever, arthritis, heart trouble, and other so-called incurable diseases which have not responded properly to treatment elsewhere."

While continuing to treat cancer, Spears Hospital became cagier in its claims. In November, 1963, *Prevention* magazine, a publication interested in unorthodox medical

---

* Spears apparently couldn't make his methods for this disease work on himself.

** When I read this, I recalled Dr. Edward T. Wentworth's comment cited in Chapter Three—"Only a strong, healthy person can afford to indulge in chiropractic treatment." Dr. Wentworth's statement went on to say, "unfortunately, there are weak and unhealthy ones who use it."

and nutritional theories, published an article on the hospital. "Suppose a cancer victim presents himself at the Spears Clinic [sic], what can be expect?" the article queries. "When asked that question, both Dr. Howard Spears and Dr. Dan Spears were quick to insist that, 'We have no cancer cure. We just put the patient on a regime of chiropractic adjustments and introduce an internal cleansing effort, including fasts, if the condition permits, frequent colonic irrigation [enemas] and elimination of sweets.'

" 'And this cures serious cancer conditions?'

" 'We do not employ the term "cure" where cancer is concerned,' said Dr. Howard Spears. 'We only know that some patients with cancers, as diagnosed by their family physicians, come here as a last resort, and walk out, apparently free from cancer.' "

When asked exactly how the treatment at Spears affects the cancer his reply, according to the article, was, "We don't know. We just pursue the general chiropractic theory, with minor modifications for the individual, and watch for results."

Spears was finally put out of the cancer business in 1964, when the state of Colorado passed a law prohibiting chiropractors from treating cancer. But there have been consolations. Spears is opening up an even bigger field—chiropractic treatment for persons with mental and emotional illness.

Among the materials I received at Spears was a mimeographed paper entitled "The Chiropractic Approach to Mental Illness," by L. M. King, a chiropractor associated with the hospital. "Various conditions within the spine," says Dr. King, "constitute the biggest single group of primary causes for depletion of nervous energy, directly or indirectly, that bring on mental as well as physical illness."

"The response of mentally ill patients to chiropractic procedures gives a firm basis for assuming some connection between cerebral blood flow and the mental state of the individual," the paper says. The thesis, in brief, is that this blood flow is controlled by nerves, and these nerves may be impinged by spinal subluxations or misalignments. This will cause the nerves to function imperfectly, the flow of blood will be diminished, and mental or emotional illness could ensue.

For example, says Dr. King, "Far oftener than is generally realized, distortions in neck posture and alignment produce disturbances of the emotions persistent and severe enough to constitute mental illness. Should the doctor be unaware of the relationship that exists between personality disorders and postural changes in the upper spine, his efforts are apt to fall short of their intended purpose."

Bad posture, he says, is one of the villains: "Poor vertebral alignment, arising from postural abnormalities, can interfere with cerebral circulation sufficiently to lay the groundwork for mental illness."

"Effective techniques for restoring mental health," says the paper, include: "spinal adjusting," especially "Spears painless system of full spine adjusting"; "motorized intermittent spinal traction"; and "colon irrigations."

As for benefits, Dr. King ticks them off:

Schizophrenia: "Results encourage the belief that chiropractic possesses the potential means for helping a greater percentage of those afflicted with this type of mental illness than is presently being done by any other therapeutic approach."

Involutional Psychosis: "The treating procedures of chiropractors restore the functional integrity of the nervous system. This restorative change holds prospects of affording relief that is more certain and permanent because it eliminates causes instead of suppressing symptoms."

The Neuroses: "The neuroses in all their many expressions respond equally well to chiropractic treatment. Most patients either completely recover or show improvement enough to be relieved of their most distressing symptoms. They are in effect enabled to achieve the cherished goal of a happier life aspired to by everyone."

Mentally ill persons, says Dr. King, should be hospitalized—at Spears. "The Spears Hospital," he says, "has treated patients with all types of mental illness. It is ideally suited for this because the atmosphere of the entire hospital radiates friendliness and helpfulness so essential to the lessening of anxiety and fear. Only in surroundings conducive to cooperation can chiropractic work the magic on disturbed minds of which it is capable."

The chiropractic world is jumping on the bandwagon. The October, 1964, issue of the *Journal of Chiropractic*, published by the American Chiropractic Association, carried an article entitled "Psychological Research Project Is Being Continued," by Herman S. Schwartz, D.C., who is identified in the article as president, Council on Psychotherapy. The article says:

> During the past year we have continued with our chiropractic psychological research project. We are of the strong opinion:
>
> "that the public should be graphically informed that chiropractic can be of distinct benefit to the emotionally disturbed, and to the more than 10 million mental casualties that occur annually;
>
> "that, when the chiropractor accepts such patients, he is definitely venturing within his rightful realm of endeavor;
>
> "that, when we do help the patient with an emotional stress situation, we accomplish it because of the neuro-psychological implications within the chiropractic adjustment."

The paperback book *Chiropractic: A Modern Way to Health* by Dr. Julius Dintenfass, D.C. (New York: Pyramid Books, 1966), devotes a whole chapter to "Facts about Emotional Illness." "Chiropractic clinical observations verify that emotional disturbances are often associated with chronic pain of the joints and muscles of the legs and arms, as well as the backbone. They clear up after the correction of the physical condition with chiropractic care."

As the juggernaut has headed in their direction, medical and scientific workers in the field of mental health have looked on with dismay. Mrs. Winthrop Rockefeller, president of the National Association for Mental Health, spoke out at the Third National Congress on Medical Quackery, jointly sponsored by the American Medical Association and the National Health Council, held in Chicago in October, 1966:

> [A] critical area for joint concern, both by the medical profession and our volunteer citizens' organization, falls under the general blanket or umbrella of treatment by people who are far beyond their skills or are simply not qualified and trained to deal with mental illness. For example, we all can look with alarm upon the growing participation of chiropractors in treating mental problems. I am not here to defend or condemn the field of chiropractics; this is already an area of professional concern and study by appropriate medical organizations. But I can unequivocally condemn the assumption by bone and joint manipulators of the psychiatric function. I think we can flatly say that the chiropractor has no business treating mental illness, and stand squarely on that statement.

Actually, if some chiropractors treat such conditions as arthritis, multiple sclerosis, and cerebral palsy under their present state-issued licenses, it is unlikely that they can be effectively prevented from carrying their adjustment tables into the field of mental illness.

And, as we shall see in the next chapter, there are other problems about which little can be done as long as chiropractors hold the status of state-licensed practitioners.

CHAPTER EIGHT

X Ray—the Chiropractor's Toy

THE PRINCIPAL MENACE TO PUBLIC HEALTH POSED BY CHIRO-practic is that it removes sick persons from scientific treatment, and thus endangers their health and sometimes their lives. But there are at least two other dangers that cannot be ignored, and these will be discussed in the following two chapters. The first of these dangers is the use of X ray by chiropractors.

Within the past few years there has been increasing concern within the medical and scientific communities about the amount of radiation to which the public is exposed by diagnostic X ray. No one minimizes the dangers; no one denies that X-radiation from any source is basically damaging; all agree that unnecessary exposure should be avoided—except some chiropractors: see the Parker seminar *Textbook*'s recommendations on what chiropractors should say if the patient evinces concern on this subject, quoted here on page 46.

In September, 1967, the Senate Commerce Committee, chaired by Senator E. L. Bartlett (D., Alaska), opened a series of hearings on ionizing radiation hazards of electronic products. Among the witnesses was Dr. Karl Z. Morgan, director of health physics at Oak Ridge National Laboratory and a pioneer in radiation protection research. Dr. Morgan told the committee that there was an urgent need for improvement in diagnostic X ray. Continued use of X rays at the present rate in a population of the nation's current size, he said, could lead to as many as 27,000 deaths a year from genetic defects, 1,100 from leukemia, and a non-specific life-shortening effect on 1,000 persons. He set forth a series of sixty-three recommendations for improving the diagnostic value of X rays while reducing the exposure of patients—and doctors—to radiation.

There is some disagreement among scientists regarding the magnitude and immediacy of the dangers posed by the use of diagnostic X ray. But reduction of the use of X ray in diagnosis to an absolute minimum, and continuing refinement of technique to cut down the amount of radiation to which the patient is exposed when diagnostic X ray is unavoidable, are unanimous objectives of modern scientific medicine.

A number of chiropractors take a different tack. They use their machines liberally in pursuit of a medically false theory of disease—and use them for public relations as much as for medical purposes. Chiropractic X ray is now probably the largest source of totally gratuitous radiation of the United States public.

No figures on actual usage are available, but the recommendations are clear:

"In my ten years of practice," the Parker *Textbook* suggests that chiropractors tell their patients, "75 percent have been fully X-rayed, 15 percent partially X-rayed, and 10 percent required no X ray at all." By contrast, X rays are used in only 3 percent of cases under medical supervision at Johns Hopkins Hospital.

Chiropractors call their X-ray technique "spinography." It consists of taking a picture 36 inches high and 14 inches wide, of the entire vertebral column, as was done to me when I visited the Palmer College of Chiropractic Clinic as a "patient." Chiropractic spinography was discussed in detail by the Quebec College of Physicians and Surgeons in a *Brief* prepared in 1963 for submission to the Quebec legislature, which was considering holding hearings on a bill to license chiropractors:

> This film is obtained with a very wide stream of radiation, which blankets almost the whole trunk of the body as it penetrates from the front to the film at the back. It is unusual for the chiropractor to take a side view, since the technical difficulties are great and the resulting film even less satisfactory than the anteroposterior view.*

This large plate gives the chiropractor a handsome full view of his chosen turf, the spine, which he can show to his patient. The chiropractor mounts it on a fluorescent screen and sections it off with two-inch squares drawn on the negative with radio-opaque ink. (The Parker Chiropractic Research Foundation also recommends that the chiropractor give the patient a "polaroid reproduction of his spinal X ray with the doctor's stamp on back." "Give it in a neat printed folder," a foundation instructor suggests. "People will show it to others.") "In theory," says the *Brief*, "the purpose of these squares is to help visualize disturbances in the longitudinal alignment of the vertebral column. This technical detail [sectioning the picture in two-inch squares] does not really provide a better demonstration of possible changes in vertebral structure, external or internal; on the contrary, it may interfere with visibility."

This, however, is a minor point. A more important issue is that "large films of this type, taken in the antero-posterior view only, have very limited diagnostic value."

---

* As the reader will recall, the Palmer clinic took two 14-by-36 plates of me, one a front and one a side view. To the extent that this may have become standard chiropractic practice since the Quebec College prepared its 1963 *Brief*, the radiation exposure of chiropractic patients has been doubled, and the problem has become twice as urgent.

In a full spine picture "the curvatures [normal or abnormal] of the vertebral column cause some degree of superimposition of the shadows of adjacent vertebrae the one on the other. The oblique direction of the X rays in relation to these curvatures causes only certain vertebrae to be clearly distinguished from their neighbors above and below; and indeed, focusing on a small area with careful aim is essential for the proper study of the outline and internal structure of each bone and of its relations to contiguous anatomical elements."

Physicians therefore do not usually use these oversize plates for evaluation of spinal conditions. "Small sectional views are of much more diagnostic value than a single broad picture, since they provide a more accurate perspective of architectural relationships; they allow the photographic density to be adjusted for each region; and they require less scatter of X rays, thereby giving a better quality of film and reducing the risk of genetic effects."

In connection with the Jerry R. England case in Louisiana in 1965, described in Chapter Six, medical specialists in many fields made affidavits regarding the relationship of the current state of knowledge in their fields to the theory and practice of chiropractic. One was Dr. Seymour F. Ochsner, associate professor of radiology at Tulane University School of Medicine, a member of the executive council of the American Roentgenary Society, chancellor of the American College of Radiology, and a member of the Louisiana Board of Nuclear Energy. Dr. Ochsner discussed chiropractic spinograph and X-ray techniques:

One of the most important contributions recent advances have made for the safety of the patient is the use of smaller fields of exposure of the human body rather than larger fields of exposure. The radiologist tries to focus X rays on the specific area of specific interest. By doing this, he protects other parts from unnecessary radiation exposure. At times, of course, one does need to obtain one or more views of particularly susceptible parts of the body, for instance

104

the human pelvis or genital organs, but every effort is made to shield these areas from radiation exposure and the use of excessively large fields for diagnosis of local condition is usually considered improper use of X rays for diagnosis. The broad field X ray is bad because it unnecessarily exposes a sensitive part of the body and the information obtained is not worth the hazards to the patient.

The average chiropractor is largely without the type of training in the use of X ray that many scientists regard as indispensable for achieving the three goals of taking meaningful pictures, interpreting them correctly, and providing protection for the patient.

"If an individual is going to set himself up as particularly knowledgeable about the use of X rays and diagnosis of disease," says Dr. Ochsner, "I think he should have at least three more years' intensive training (beyond the medical school curriculum) devoted almost entirely to the use of X rays and this includes a study of how X rays are produced, what effect they have on the human body, how they produce a readable X-ray film in various diseases, and also, of course, a study of the effect of X ray on human tissue, and even more specifically a study of and consideration of possible dangers of radiation to tissues. It's extremely important, I think, in doing anything to a human being in order to achieve a diagnosis to be certain that one does not injure a human being. So, the study of the possible ill effects and understanding the dangers of the use of the X ray are very important. This, I think, will take at least three years of intensive training in an individual who already knows a lot about disease and a lot about anatomy, physiology, and pathology."

The ignorance of many chiropractors about this sophisticated equipment was highlighted in a 1961 lawsuit in which the Chiropractic Association of New York, on behalf of itself, its individual members, and a chiropractor named Ernest E. Quatro, sought to force the New York State Public Health Commissioner to permit chiropractors to use X-ray machines. The practice of chiropractic was at that time not licensed in New York State. In his decision upholding the State Public Health Commissioner's refusal to permit chiropractic use of X ray, the judge listed 152 Findings of Fact. They included:

> The plaintiff Quatro used no cone on his X-ray machine nor did he use any other instrumentality or device for the purpose of shielding or protecting the patient from the primary X-ray beam or from scatter.
>
> . . .
>
> The plaintiff Quatro as of the time he was exposing the lumbar and sacral areas of the spine of his patients to ionizing radiation was not aware of the very great danger to the reproductive organs of the male and female resulting from such exposure.

In the following year New York State passed a law licensing chiropractors and permitting their use of X rays. Alone among the states, New York also passed, in 1966, a law requiring all X-ray machine operators to be licensed and to pass an examination to show at least minimum proficiency in operation of the equipment. It seems likely that in the other forty-nine states of the Union there are many chiropractors—busy irradiating their patients—who have no greater knowledge of their equipment than that displayed by Dr. Quatro in his 1961 testimony.

Once the chiropractor has his X-ray plate marked and mounted, he almost always finds "subluxations" of one or more vertebrae of his patients, which radiologists, neurologists, orthopedists, rheumatologists, and psychiatrists, are somehow unable to see or do not know how to see. One explanation may be that the chiropractor's knowledge of medicine exceeds that of such specialists, but that seems unlikely. Another possibility is suggested by the Quebec College *Brief:* "The 'subluxations' to which they refer are not the same as those defined in classical medical terms."

If the chiropractor chooses to designate any deviation

from complete symmetry as a "subluxation," the *Brief* makes it clear that he will have no problems, since a perfectly symmetrical picture of the spine would probably be difficult to take. Any slight deviation of the patient's posture from the perfect vertical as the X-ray picture is taken will show on the film as "displacements of articular surfaces one upon the other." Although these are phenomena of normal movement, the patient can be told that they are pathological conditions when they are caught on film by the X-ray candid camera. Since the chiropractor regards subluxations as being, by definition, extremely minute variations, it would probably be a rare X-ray plate on which he was not home free.

For patients beyond the first blush of youth the chiropractor does not even have to depend on normal body movement to get his subluxations. Dr. James M. Morris, assistant professor of orthopedic surgery at the University of California Medical Center, says that changes in spinal discs "due to degeneration begin at about twenty years of age and increase progressively throughout life."

"After the age of forty," says the Quebec College *Brief*, "perfectly normal vertebral columns become rapidly rarer. It is unusual after that age to see spines without X-ray evidence of aging, including thinning of the discs and thinning and slipping of articular surfaces. . . . The longer a man lives the more impressive the radiologic changes in his vertebral column become."

And, of course, even this fails to reach the ultimate question. Where is the proof that these spinal "subluxations," real or imaginary, are pinching nerves? The *Brief* comments succinctly: "Over and above all this is the undeniable fact that 'spinography,' i.e., the single X ray of the whole spine on which chiropractors rely, has never demonstrated the pinching of a nerve, since nerves are not visible on X-ray films and can only be demonstrated by the injection of liquid or gaseous contrast media . . . in many more serious and extensive diseases of the vertebral column, it is necessary to inject into the spinal canal a substance opaque to X ray [a technique which chiropractors do not use] so that a highly trained specialist may achieve an accurate diagnosis of the location of the pathologic process. Chiropractors, with lesser means, claim a greater precision of diagnosis. But here again, no scientific proof supports the claim."

The results obtained by chiropractors through this method of analyzing illness are not scientifically viable. Dr. Ochsner, commenting on a chiropractic textbook that teaches the techniques and uses of spinography, states:

The chiropractic manual entitled *Textbook of Logan Basic Methods,* edited from the original manuscript of Hugh B. Logan, D.C., by Vinton F. Logan and Fern F. Murray, illustrates some of the so-called "spinograph" films apparently used by chiropractors for diagnosis or "analysis." These films purport to be "before and after" X rays relative to various diseases such as appendicitis, asthma, back injury, constipation, diabetes, irregular menses, nervous breakdown, "disabled by pain," prostate disorder, sciatica, sciatic rheumatism, migraine headaches, heart condition, ear and throat abscesses, pain in kidneys, and lumbago and sciatica. The only comment that radiologists could make about these films is that the quality is very poor and the apparent diagnoses made on the basis of the films are completely ridiculous.

Actually, more than just medical considerations seem to be involved in the use of X ray by some chiropractors. In some instances, X ray is apparently used as the keystone of a program to update their public image and assume the appearance of practicing scientific healing.

Chiropractic literature on the subject includes a book called *Modern X-Ray Practice and Chiropractic Spinography* by P. A. Remier, listed in the 1965–1966 catalog of the Palmer College of Chiropractic as professor of X ray and chairman of the department of X ray. In addition to the alleged usefulness of X ray for chiropractic analysis, the text says that "reasons why the chiropractor should spinograph every case" include:

IT PROMOTES CONFIDENCE

IT CREATES INTEREST AMONG PATIENTS

IT PROCURES BUSINESS

IT ATTRACTS A BETTER CLASS OF PATIENTS

IT ADDS PRESTIGE IN YOUR COMMUNITY

IT BUILDS A RELIABLE REPUTATION

IT IS AN INVESTMENT AND NOT AN EXPENSE

IT PROVIDES GOOD INTEREST ON YOUR INVESTMENT

IT HELPS TO ELIMINATE THE SO-CALLED STARVATION PERIOD THAT MANY PRACTITIONERS GO THROUGH

The Parker Seminar *Textbook* agrees. Reasons for doing a full-spine X ray, the book says, include "Psychological," "Financial," "Reputation."

Practitioners of scientific medicine use X ray only when no other method of examination will reveal problems or pathology. "The thesis on which we operate," said a medical expert in the Quatro court action, "is [that] radiation is undesirable and hence the clinical indications for the taking of a film or series of films must be established beforehand." By contrast, the Parker-system chiropractor X-rays the patient *as soon as he consents to an examination, and before any examination of the patient has been made;* the very first thing that happens to a patient who says "yes" is that he gets a 14-by-36-inch dose.

The chiropractor following the Parker technique not only X-rays early, he X-rays often. During the period of the first ten adjustments, discussed in an earlier chapter, the Parker *Textbook* advises the chiropractor to "Take small comparative X ray for some particular problem that's not progressing exactly as it should and perhaps make no charge." After that, he should "Re-X-ray if necessary (active patients, every three months; once-a-month patients, once each year)." It seems likely that the chiropractor will find it necessary. The *Textbook* presumes that

109

more pictures will be taken. "Talk enthusiastically about the results you are getting," it says. "Show evidence of results. Show before and after heart graphs, X rays, etc." "There isn't a spine that shouldn't be X-rayed once a year," Parker told the seminar.

The chiropractor is advised to use his X-ray machine in his campaign to keep current patients and get new ones. The *Textbook* suggests that he print up handsome little cards—"Lifetime X-ray cards, three-year X-ray cards, one-year X-ray cards," entitling the bearers to free X rays during the period designated on the card. The cards are then judiciously distributed: "Give current satisfied patients an annual X-ray card with the name of a friend or loved one on it as a quick referral stimulus."

In the author's opinion, the use of X ray in pursuit of the chiropractic theory of disease should be banned in every state in the Union, for reasons of public safety and public health.

CHAPTER NINE

The Hands of
Danger and Death

Spinal manipulation is dangerous?
Answer: MYTH.
Spinal manipulation is perfectly safe when
done by a competent chiropractic specialist.

—*Fact or Myth: A Quiz on Health
Care*, booklet issued by the American Chiropractic Association.

IN ADDITION TO THE DANGERS OF CHIROPRACTIC X RAY,
chiropractic treatment itself can pose direct threats to
health and life. A small but inexorable number of people
are directly killed by chiropractic adjustments. Another,
and larger, group is either directly injured by adjustments,
or is suffering from a condition that is aggravated and
harmed by chiropractic treatment.

In connection with the Jerry R. England case in Louisiana, a number of medical specialists provided affidavits
regarding the relationship of chiropractic to their various
specialties, which included pathology, bacteriology,
physiology, anatomy, neurology, surgery, radiology,

111

orthopedic surgery, physical medicine, and internal medicine. Several of these affidavits discussed the dangers of chiropractic treatment.

The experts noted that manipulation *does* occasionally find a place among the methods of therapy used in scientific medical treatment. "In the area of physical medicine," said Dr. Solomon D. Winokur, a diplomate of the American Academy of Physical Medicine and a specialist in physical medicine and rehabilitation, "manipulation is an integral part of the treatment of conditions arising from the vertebral structures, producing pain within the areas of the vertebral structures at a distant point, either by nerve root irritation or producing restriction of motion within the vertebral structures themselves."

First of all, however, "successful and safe manipulation is possible only where a complete and accurate diagnosis is made. The knowledge and skill for such a diagnosis can come only from extensive training in a well-accredited medical school."

Second, "the conditions [for which manipulation would be the correct treatment] are a very small proportion of all the things a doctor might see . . . manipulation of the vertebral column has a very limited place in the overall treatment of disability and disease that occur in human beings."

Third, "manipulation of the vertebral column is potentially dangerous and harmful." Dr. Winokur illustrated the point in detail:

In patients who have a malignant disease of the structure, not only can fractures be produced by manipulation, but dislocation in conjunction with this sufficient to cause paraplegic or quadriplegic, depending on what section of the lower back is manipulated. Similar dislocations are also possible from forceful manipulation for the diseases such as prostatis, appendix, gall bladder, etc., which . . . also produce pain in the back.

112

Readers will recall that all three of these diseases are among those mentioned in chiropractic literature as conditions that chiropractors can and do treat.

Manipulation of the neck is particularly dangerous. At the neck region the spinal cord may actually be severed or sufficiently compressed so that the patient becomes completely disabled below the area of the pressure. In addition to these severe effects of manipulation of the neck, the other aftereffects I personally see are that the surrounding structures are so traumatized that the residual pain is far more severe than the original pain for which they were manipulated.

As I read this I remembered the sharp manipulations of my neck and head that had been given to me at the Palmer College and National College clinics, and I counted my blessings. In view of the symptomology I presented, and the treatment I received, at Palmer, I was interested in Dr. Winokur's comments on disc troubles and low-back adjustments. "It is equally possible to create permanent disability in the low-back area with manipulation," he states. "Manipulation of a slipped disc in the low-back region where the diagnosis has been missed and proper precautions not taken can produce enough compression of the spinal cord to render the patient a paraplegic. The most common type of disc problem, a fragment of the disc protruding posteriorly or laterally enough to cause nerve compression, simply is not amenable to manipulation. They just will not go back in; because if they were going back in, they would have gone in of their own accord."

Additional points were added by Dr. Irvin Cahen, professor and head of the orthopedic department of Louisiana State University Medical School. Instead of moving body structures by manipulation, Dr. Cahen said, we would prefer the patient to move the affected joint . . . considerable caution must be maintained in this passive approach [of manipulation by the doctor instead of movement by the patient]. . . . Because of this, our specialty, while accepting manipulation as a technique, places considerable limitations upon its usage. . . . I hesitate to utilize manipulations of the vertebral spine unless I'm certain that such manipulation can basically be performed by the patient's individual muscular reactions. A patient who takes calisthenics will gradually mobilize his spine within his ability, as contrasted to an excessive force that could be applied by the manipulator.

Related problems were emphasized by Dr. Philip H. Jones, emeritus professor of clinical medicine at Louisiana State University and editor of the *Journal of the Louisiana State Medical Society*. "The chiropractor is potentially dangerous," said Dr. Jones, "because the force is applied in such a way as to give the patient insufficient time to muster his own defensive vascular physical mechanisms."

Actual maladies created by chiropractic adjustments were discussed by Dr. Richard M. Paddison, professor of neurology at Louisiana State University School of Medicine and chief of the Electroencephalographic Laboratory, Southern Baptist Hospital in New Orleans:

Chiropractic manipulation is not without its hazards. There are well-documented medical cases of serious disorder to the cervical spine, cervical disc, cerebellum, spinal cord or to the cerebral arteries which ascend through the formaina or transverse sarium in the cervical vertebrae, all of which are therefore subject to be bruised and injured with forceful manipulation. There are also well-documented cases of occlusion of cerebral vessels and injury to the brain stem which involves a key area for regulation of the head and neck and an area through which all important outgoing stimulae from the nervous system or incoming sensory data are fed. Such thrombotic lesions are productive of grave and permanent neurological defects, either by infection of the brain stem or stricture by injury to the arteries which supply these vital regions.

Dr. Paddison's statements are fully supported by case histories in medical journals and by court records. The March, 1963, issue of the *Wisconsin Medical Journal* carried a case report by Robert A. Pribek, M.D., of serious brain damage to a man whose neck had been adjusted by a chiropractor. The bibliography following his article cited ten other cases of injuries following head and neck manipulation that had been reported in medical journals between 1947 and 1963. Four of these injuries had been fatal.

Without conducting any search for such cases, but simply in the process of doing research for other chapters of this book, I came across three more. One was a California decision involving a death, reported in the *Journal of the American Medical Association* in 1940; the second was a serious spinal injury reported in the January, 1943, issue of the *Kentucky Medical Journal;* the third was a 1953 court action involving a death. It seems likely that a search of hospital records and court records throughout the land would produce others.

The California case involved a six-year-old boy. The mother's testimony in the court action is summarized in the following three paragraphs.

She said he told her that it had been painful for him to stand fully erect since another child had bumped him in school. Soon he added another complaint—his legs were feeling weak. His parents took him to a chiropractor, who X-rayed the child and stated that the trouble stemmed from a subluxated vertebra. He put the youngster on a regimen of chiropractic adjustments, one every three days.

115

After four or five adjustments the boy developed a temperature of about 100°. He lost weight, vitality, and color, complained of pain during the adjustments, and began to experience paralysis in his legs and arms.

The mother discussed her son's condition with the chiropractor. He assured her that it was not necessary to bring a medical doctor in on the case, because "the only thing the boy had was a certain pressure on the spinal cord, on account of the misplaced vertebra, and he was doing the best thing, and nothing more could be done for the child." He kept up the adjustments for four months, at the end of which time the child died.

In the court action the chiropractor stated that he had found in the boy's spine a "subluxation of the second cervical vertebra, impinging the nerves, and causing a congestion in the cord," as well as a "rotation of the second, third and fourth cervical." He testified in part as follows:

Q: Did you make any diagnosis of his condition at that time?

A: In chiropractic, we don't use the term "diagnosis." I take it that you want to know if I placed a name on his condition?

Q: Yes. I want to know if you came to a conclusion?

A: Yes, I came to a conclusion, but in chiropractic we term it "analysis" instead of "diagnosis." . . . My analysis was that he had a subluxation of the second cervical vertebra, causing an impingement of the nerves at that point.

Q: Well, was that an impingement of the nerves or of the cord?

A: Well, it might have been from both. It was apparent from his condition that there was inflammation of the cord. The inflammation might have been from pressure on the spinal nerves, or upon the cord itself.

Q: So, it was your finding and your conclusion that at all times, from the time of your first treatment

to the last, there was some inflammation and congestion of the spinal cord at the region of the cervical
vertebrae?

A: Yes.

A doctor associated with the county coroner's office testified that the autopsy he performed on the boy's body
"showed the body thin, the lungs congested, the left lung
being pneumonic, and both lungs studded with small
tubercles. . . . There was no evidence of spinal or other
injury. . . . I had been informed that there was some
spinal condition existing, and I therefore examined the
spine to see if I could find any abnormality, which I did
not find."

This doctor and another called to testify stated that
the child was apparently suffering from meningitis, and
the second doctor added that the condition probably included secondary tuberculosis of the spine. Asked what
effect chiropractic adjustment of the second cervical vertebra would have in such a case, the doctor who performed the autopsy replied, "It would be detrimental, as
rest and quiet would be absolutely indicated in those
cases." Adjustments, he stated, would accelerate or increase the existing inflammation.

Both doctors agreed that chiropractic treatment in such
a case not only harmed the child by keeping him away
from proper treatment, but was in itself contraindicated.
If the child had had correct medical attention, they said,
his chances of recovery would have been good. The jury
found the chiropractor guilty of malpractice, and awarded
the mother $10,000.*

---

* This case compares interestingly with the Marvin Phillips case
(see Prologue). A generation later, Los Angeles County Deputy
District Attorney John Miner, confronted with a situation that has
many elements in common with this one, brought not a malpractice action but a charge of second-degree murder. The case above
strongly emphasizes Miner's contention that, until the Phillips
case, the penalties for utter irresponsibility toward human life in
the field of health have been grotesquely trivial.

In the Kentucky case a woman was admitted to a hospital the day after she had had a chiropractic adjustment of her lower spine. Following the adjustment, a swelling developed over her buttocks and she suffered loss of control of her bowels. An operation was performed under the direction of a neurosurgeon, and it was found that the fifth lumbar disc was almost completely ruptured.

In the 1953 Missouri case, a Missouri housewife had been suffering from a stiff neck, eye trouble, and occasional headaches. She went to the family doctor who gave her a full examination. The stiff neck, he said, was due to a muscular strain, and the headaches were caused by her need for eyeglasses. Apparently dubious, she went to a chiropractor with her husband. The latter's testimony at the trial was as follows:

The chiropractor told her that she had some misplaced vertebrae. Placing her face-down on his chiropractic table, he began to adjust her spine, moving up toward her neck. Then, asking her to step off the table, he changed it to a vertical position, and told her to stand in front of the table, facing it. He took her head in his hands and moved it sharply, first in one direction and then in the other. Each time something popped, and the woman screamed. "I'm falling," she said several times, but the chiropractor continued to manipulate her neck.

After the adjustment the chiropractor and the woman's husband helped her to a chair. She was unable to hold her head up, her hands and face were numb, and she began to vomit. She said that she felt no pain but she appeared to be in convulsions. She was helped to a cot where she continued to vomit and seemed to be without control of her movements. At this point the chiropractor called a medical doctor. The doctor recommended that the woman be taken to a hospital, which was done; but she did not respond to treatment and died about eighteen hours later.

An autopsy revealed no condition that could have

caused her death other than the injury inflicted by the chiropractic adjustment. The injury was one to the spinal meninges resulting in intraspinal bleeding and compression of the spinal cord.

The examination failed to show any displacement of any vertebrae.

Perhaps the most chilling aspect of the case was the testimony of two chiropractors who were called as expert witnesses by the defense. Both testified that the defendant had done nothing in his treatment of the woman that was not in accordance with the accepted practice of chiropractors generally in that community.

Head and neck adjustments probably pose the greatest physical dangers to patients. All eleven cases covered in Dr. Robert A. Pribek's *Wisconsin Medical Journal* article and its bibliography involved this type of manipulation. One of the references in the bibliography is to an article by Doctors Roger A. Smith and Montgomery N. Estridge, reporting two cases in the November 3, 1962, issue of the *Journal of the American Medical Association.* They state that head manipulation "can be fraught with real dangers and even result in death. Serious damage to the underlying nervous system can be inflicted by less than vigorous adjustments of the head."

One of their two cases was that of a thirty-three-year-old woman who developed stiffness and pain in her neck. She sought out a chiropractor and was given an adjustment of the head without ill effect. About a week later, however, when she was given a second adjustment of the head and neck, she suddenly developed nausea, vomiting, and vertigo, and lost coordination in her arms and legs. She was hospitalized the same day. A physician visited her and noted that she was somewhat drowsy, although she could be easily aroused. The original symptoms, however, persisted. Her drowsiness increased, her blood pressure rose, and within about eight hours she went into a coma and her breathing stopped. She was put in an artificial respirator and rushed to surgery. The operation revealed rupture and herniation of the cerebellar cortex. After the operation her condition remained unchanged, and three days later she died.

To physicians and surgeons, the wonder of the matter is not that there are so many such injuries reported but that there are so few. In an article in the May 30, 1959, issue of the *Journal of the American Medical Association* that reports two cases, Robert J. Joynt, M.D., and David Green, M.B., of the State University of Iowa Department of Neurology, speculate that only persons with large vascular arteries leading to the brain are notably susceptible to such accidents. This explanation, they said, seems most likely to account for "the rarity of brain-stem vascular accidents after manipulations in a population which is overly exposed to such treatment."

The theme is picked up by Doctors Smith and Estridge in their 1962 article. "The ideal treatment in these cases is prophylactic [preventive]," they state. "Can there be some practical method of determining which patients are susceptible to vascular embarrassment to the brain stem following head manipulation?" For persons receiving chiropractic treatment it could be a life-saving question, but I found no interest in the matter registered in any of the large volume of chiropractic literature I read in the course of writing this book.

A number of medical doctors have told me alarming stories about patients they have treated who were first treated by chiropractors. Typical is the case encountered by a doctor who described it to me with the patient's record folder open in front of him.

In April, 1965, he was visited by a lady who was accompanied by her grown daughter. The lady stated that she had been suffering for about three months from a pain in her lower back, going down into her left hip and leg. She visited a chiropractor who had a ground-floor office in a building on the same block as the office of the doctor, less than a hundred yards away.

The chiropractor X-rayed her, told her she had some subluxations, and started her on a series of adjustments. The lady found, however, that her condition did not improve, and she decided to seek a medical doctor's opinion.

The symptoms, the doctor said in describing the case to me, "were highly suggestive of an orthopedic problem in the lower back."

With the lady and her daughter sitting there, my doctor called the chiropractor on the phone and asked if he might have the X rays that the chiropractor had made.

"I can't do it now," the chiropractor replied, "I'm about to go out."

"I'm just down the block from you," the doctor replied. "The lady's daughter is sitting here. She'll run right over and pick them up from you."

"I have no time for that," the chiropractor said.

The lady's daughter nevertheless jumped up and ran down the block to the chiropractor's office, arriving there within moments after the phone conversation. She pounded on the chiropractor's door and rang the bell. There was no reply. It was a ground-floor office; the young lady looked in the window and saw that the chiropractor was there. But he would not let her in; and he never provided the X rays.

The doctor sent the patient to an orthopedic specialist. He X-rayed the woman and found that her fifth lumbar vertebra was fractured and the intervening disc space had been narrowed. The treatment she received was the exact opposite of that given by the chiropractor; instead of being vigorously manipulated, her back was immobilized and she underwent a period of bed rest.

The woman had tripped on the steps of her church just before the pain began, and had had no accidents between then and the time she was X-rayed by the orthopedist. There are really only two major possibilities. Either the woman's back was already fractured and her disc compressed when she went to the chiropractor, and he failed to comprehend his X rays; or she had a lesser condition when she went to him, and he damaged her back.*

Perhaps most tragic of all is the injury and death that chiropractors can inflict on their own children by delaying proper medical treatment. "I have been able to obtain and review the chart of a chiropractor's child who died at Charity Hospital in New Orleans," say Dr. Richard M. Paddison. In his affidavit made for use in the England case, Dr. Paddison said, "This child [was] presented at one of the private hospitals in town; the parents were told it had meningitis. The father preferred to take it home to treat it. The child was returned to the private hospital [some time later] in relative extremis. A spinal puncture was then performed under the father's protest and it was found that this child was suffering from hemaphelus influenza meningitis. In spite of the prompt institution of vigorous and intensive antibiotic therapy, the child died."

Of course, people also die under medical care. The issue is whether there is a responsible application of scientific medical knowledge. On the question of the validity of chiropractic, let us first hear from chiropractors and chiropractic groups in Chapter Ten, and then turn to the views of medical researchers and scientists in Chapter Eleven.

---

* At Palmer College Clinic I presented the same syndrome of symptomatology. In neither instance did the chiropractors show any sign of recognizing its possible meaning, either in my case where the condition did not exist, or in the woman's case where some kind of condition did exist.

CHAPTER TEN

"But It Works!"
—Or Does It?

A MIDWEST CHIROPRACTOR RECENTLY PLACED AN ADVERtisement in a newspaper that read in part:

> This 66-year-old lady had suffered from diabetes for
> 21 years. . . . She had taken insulin over a period of
> time and had learned to live with the condition.
> After several adjustments she became aware that she
> no longer needed insulin, and is happy to report
> that a backache pain between her shoulders that once
> kept her miserable is now no longer a problem.

As we have seen, some chiropractors, unlike medical
doctors, advertise by publishing testimonials of persons
who have supposedly been helped or cured by chiropractic treatment.

It should be noted, to begin with, that personal testimonials are not used in scientific medicine to prove or
disprove the validity of therapies, and for good reason.
There has probably never been a worthless or fraudulent
treatment that could not produce a legion of persons who

would swear that it helped or cured them. Nothing could be more impressive than to pore over old files on phony and often tragically dangerous remedies and treatments and to see in these files the reams of statements from persons who say that the remedy delivered them from their illness after everything else had failed. The statements were undoubtedly given freely, and represent the true belief of the persons who gave them. In some instances they are notarized, or were given under oath in court.

Some of the reasons behind such testimonials have been commented on by Dr. Richard M. Paddison. "The average human being is simply not competent to judge accurately the value of any therapeutic treatment," he says. An important factor which the person cannot assess, he says, is, "Was the result actually in response to the treatment?"

Again, there is the fact that psychological considerations play a powerful role. "Individuals who are particularly psychiatrically susceptible to suggestion and persuasion," he states, "often readily give up their symptoms under the influence of counseling and reassuring." The same thing can be true even with less susceptible persons. "It has been noted that with scientifically sophisticated people like medical students, if given pills which are known to be biologically inert along with the advice and suggestion that they will produce adverse effects, such as cramps, diarrhea, nausea and vomiting, 25 to 40 percent may report the adverse effects; and conversely, if they are told that these pills will have a very beneficial effect in keeping them from catching cold, then similarly they will swear that these pills have protected them from colds all winter."

Again, some diseases are characterized by spontaneous remissions—that is to say, they come and go. Multiple sclerosis and rheumatoid arthritis are two such diseases. It is noteworthy that "improvement" of these conditions is prominently featured in chiropractic patient testimonials.

Another factor that probably accounts for many chiropractic "cures" is that many or most symptoms are self-limiting. In laymen's language, a condition will in most cases get only so bad, then it will improve, in whole or in part, temporarily or permanently. To get a favorable testimonial, all one has to do is to ask the person, at the right time, whether or not he feels better. Chiropractic treatment, says Dr. Milton Helpern, Chief Medical Examiner of the City of New York, "caters to and exploits those individuals who are afflicted with symptoms which are self-limited and if the timing is right seem to respond to their manipulations. It apparently succeeds in situations in which a patient's complaints do not respond to immediate care of the physician but eventually prove self-limiting coincidental with chiropractic manipulation."

Unfortunately, even more serious issues are raised by some chiropractic testimonials.

A leading user of testimonials is Spears Chiropractic Hospital. Its publication, the *Sanigram,* and various other booklets and leaflets issued by the hospital, are full of stories, pictures, and statements of patients who have allegedly been helped by the hospital's treatment.

When Spears sued the Denver Better Business Bureau, the Denver *Post,* and some eighty other parties for libel in the 1950's, the records and case histories of numerous persons appearing in Spears's testimonials were introduced into evidence. According to the records, some patients whose glowing statements appeared in Spears's literature were dead when the material was published.

A Spears's circular entitled "Good News," bearing a postmark of December 29, 1953, was among the exhibits. Producing actual death certificates, the defense stated that one person whose testimonial appeared in this publication had died November 9, 1950; another, in December, 1952; a third, in June, 1953; a fourth in December, 1953.

Among other cases was that of John M. Parsons.* The Spears *Sanigram* for August, 1953, carried an item entitled "Spears Treatment Relieves Cancer; Patient Still Has Lung and Health." The item read:

---

* The victim's name is fictional, though the victim is not.

John M. Parsons is one lung and years of health ahead since arrestment of his cancer at SPEARS hospital.

He suffered from shortness of breath which assumed such serious aspects that he consulted a doctor who had no trouble diagnosing his patient's malady: A slow-growing tumor affected the bronchial tube which supplied air on that side. A biopsy proved the tumor to be malignant. Various orthodox practitioners took X rays of Mr. Parsons' ailing lung, and all came to the same conclusion—that surgery was the only recourse. . . .

Mr. Parsons meditated on his situation briefly. He told the surgeon he would have "to think it over." He visited [a chiropractor] who recommended that the sick man go to SPEARS, since the malady was far advanced. Mr. Parsons accepted this advice. He was admitted to SPEARS March 23, 1953, very ill, weak, depressed, and gasping for air. His heart was overworked as a result of operating on "one lung power."

Within slightly less than four weeks, Mr. Parsons' blocked lung began to function. As it improved, the sped-up heart labored less and breathing became normal.

As matters transpired, the Californian checked out of SPEARS with two good lungs and one excellent heart during May, 1953. He found his recovery hard to believe, but X rays prove the cancerous growth is gone, the bronchial tube clear.

Said Mr. Parsons as he was about to leave SPEARS: "Brother! Am I happy over the way things turned out."

The man's wife wrote the following letter to the Denver Better Business Bureau:

I regret to inform you that Mr. Parsons passed away on September 8, 1953.

He went to Spears Clinic in Denver on the advice of [a chiropractor], and his treatment consisted of a special diet, and massages on his chest and back for the purpose of inflating his infected lung. Needless to say, these treatments did no good. Mr. Parsons felt worse when he came back then he did when he arrived at that institution. He also took additional treatments from [the chiropractor] when he came home with the same results.

He never did feel any better. His death came September 8, 1953.

Another type of "proof" used by chiropractors is the so-called "cure chart." These charts are circulated by many chiropractors among their patients, are used in chiropractic advertising, and are part of the standard tool kit used by chiropractic lobbies to secure legislation favorable to the chiropractic profession. They are scientific-appearing compilations supposedly showing the high percentage of persons suffering from various afflictions who have been helped by chiropractic treatment.

One of them, based on "studies reported by the Chiropractic Research Foundation of the National Chiropractic Association, the Committee on Research of the International Chiropractors Association, and Parker Chiropractic Research Foundation," includes the following:

CONDITIONS	PERCENTAGE WELL OR MUCH IMPROVED UNDER CHIROPRACTIC TREATMENT
Allergies	87.2
Anemia	81.5
Arthritis	73.5
Asthma	80.5
Constipation	79.2
Emotional disorders	85.5
Gall bladder disorders	80.9
Goiter	85.7
High blood pressure	73.0

Insomnia	81.8
Kidney disorders	81.9
Liver disorders	80.5
Menopause disorders	73.4
Migraine headaches	86.6
Paralysis	68.8
Sinusitis	83.2
Stomach disorders	82.5
Ulcers	80.2

When another chiropractic cure chart, entitled *Field Research Data,* published by the Research Committee of the International Chiropractors Association, was submitted to the Massachusetts Legislature in 1956 as part of the chiropractic lobby's intensive (and ultimately successful) efforts to get licensure in that state, Dr. Robert W. Buck, appointed by the Legislative Research Council to study the data, reported:

> This booklet might easily be accepted by the uncritical reader as a "story of chiropractic achievement," as claimed in the preface. Actually, it consists of 91 "survey sheets," each page showing by means of tables and diagrams that chiropractic treatment over periods extending from 1 to 225 days "cured" or "relieved" an average of 92 percent of all symptoms or diseases treated. This would truly seem to be an achievement until one remembers that any symptom or complaint that a patient might have is bound either to disappear or become less troublesome at some time between 1 and 225 days after it appears, at least 92 times out of 100, whether the patient has received any treatment or not. Consequently, charts of this sort could easily be prepared for any symptom or any disease under any treatment whatsoever, or under no treatment at all. *

---

* "Report submitted by the Legislative Research Council relative to boards of registration for chiropractors, electrologists, and sanatarians" (Boston, February 21, 1956) p. 85.

Chiropractors use yet another type of testimonial—statements by certain medical doctors attesting to the value of chiropractic treatment. Such a testimonial appears in the attractive booklet "Fact or Myth: A Quiz on Health Care," recently published by the American Chiropractic Association:

Buried in the pages of medical journals [the booklet states] are thousands of expressions of opinion by medical doctors indicating their confidence in the methods and principles of chiropractic. Typical is the statement made by Herman Rubin, M.D., a Fellow of the American Association for the Advancement of Science, in his book EUGENICS. "It may never occur to them [his medical colleagues] that the headaches, stomach trouble, neuritis or nervous irritability they are attempting to cure may be due to nothing more serious than a displaced vertebra which any competent chiropractor can restore in 10 seconds."

Dr. Rubin's testimonial is also cited in both of the recently published paperback books extolling chiropractic, which were mentioned in Chapter Two. An abbreviated version of it appears in the chapter entitled "Medical and Lay Opinions in Favor of Chiropractic," in Thorp McClusky's book *Your Health and Chiropractic.* An extended version appears in the chapter entitled "Progressive M.D.'s Approve Chiropractic," in *Chiropractic: A Modern Way to Health,* by Julius Dintenfass, D.C. Because of this wide dissemination, the testimonial and its author are worthy of study.

Dr. Dintenfass' book and the ACA booklet both state that Dr. Rubin is a Fellow of the American Association for the Advancement of Science. According to the American Association for the Advancement of Science, this statement is not true; Dr. Rubin is not a Fellow of the association. This group states that it does name certain persons as Fellows in recognition of their scientific achievements, but Dr. Rubin has never been named as a Fellow. He *is* a member of the association. There are no requirements for membership; anyone may join.

The ACA booklet and both paperback books give the title of Dr. Rubin's book as *Eugenics*. This is a bowdlerization. The correct title is *Eugenics and Sex Harmony*. It was published by Pioneer Publishing Company in 1934. Sections of the book bear such titles as "Secrets of the Honeymoon," "The Kiss," "The Real Reason Men Prefer Blondes," and "How to Regain Virility." There are numerous line-drawing illustrations in the text with captions such as "The Kiss," "The 'It' Girl," and "The Happy Home and the Sordid Nightclub."

The sentence quoted in the ACA booklet is an edited and shortened version of the sentence that actually appears in the book, with the chiropractor-editors giving no indication to the reader of the booklet that this has been done. The editing completely conceals the fact that Dr. Rubin's attack is *not* directed against medical doctors as the parenthetical insertion in the booklet states, but against psychoanalysts. Psychoanalysts, says Dr. Rubin, "ignore the fact that almost 90 percent of the physical ailments of mankind are due to auto-intoxication from intestinal absorption, from violation of fundamental hygienic laws, from lack of fresh air and exercise, from improper eating or from food stuffing, from faulty habits of sex life—in fact, from anything that violates any of Nature's laws." Other things that psychoanalysts may be ignoring, Dr. Rubin continues, include "hollow teeth," "focal abscesses in various structures of the body," and "the wrong kind of bath."

All this leads up to the sentence quoted in the ACA booklet. Here is how it actually reads in Dr. Rubin's book. Material omitted by the chiropractor-editors is indicated by italics.

It may never occur to them that the headaches, stomach trouble, neuritis, or nervous irritability they are attempting to cure may be due to nothing more serious than a displaced vertebra, which any competent *osteopath or* chiropractor can restore *to normal position* in ten seconds, *and which all the king's horses and all the king's men could not put back by mental means in ten years, or ten thousand years.*

Dr. Herman H. Rubin was born in Russia in 1891. He graduated from Long Island College Hospital in 1915 and was licensed in that year to practice medicine in New York State. In the early 1920's he was medical director of a firm called Gotham Corporation, which marketed an obesity remedy called Citrophan. Ads for the product stated, "Science has found that the chief cause of obesity lies in the *development of alcohol in the digestive tract,* brought about by the action of *yeast bacteria*—taken into the stomach in improperly baked bread—and on raw fruit and vegetables." An article on Citrophan in the March 1, 1924, issue of the *Journal of the American Medical Association* labels this statement untrue, and calls Citrophan "another 'fat cure' nostrum."

According to the *Journal* article, Dr. Rubin had some interesting associates in this venture. One was Edwin F. Bowers, who represented himself as an M.D. on his stationery. A "report" on Citrophan by "Dr." Bowers was used as an important part of the advertising campaign for the product. Actually, says the *Journal,* "Bowers is not a graduate in medicine, never attended any medical college as a student of medicine and is not licensed to practice medicine in any state of the Union." He was previously involved in promotions for two other patent remedies, "Bioplasm" and "Neutroids," which the *Journal* describes bluntly as fakes.

Another party in the promotion was Albert Freeman, who busied himself selling stock in Gotham. In letters to prospects he confided that "there is a large profit in Citrophan," and that he expected the company to be doing $5 million annually in a "reasonably short time." He urged prospects to buy in at $100 a share, adding, "You may send your subscription to me for the Gotham Corporation, but do not send it through a broker. . . ."

A third luminary, the *Journal* reported, was Frederick L. Childs, vice-president of Gotham. This name, says the article in the *AMA Journal*, appears in AMA's files as one who used to live at Kalamazoo, Michigan, and was vice-president of a "consumption cure" promotion and also a part owner of a Kalamazoo patent medicine concern.

After a while, Citrophan faded. Meanwhile Dr. Rubin had developed a new enthusiasm—a device called the Radiendocrinator. It consisted of a gold-plated metal wafer three-eighths of an inch thick, two inches wide, and three inches long, which was supposed to be "worn on the body over the endocrine glands while asleep." Dr. Rubin wrote a small book plugging the device, entitled *The New Science of Radiendocrinology in Its Relation to Rejuvenation*. "The Radiendocrinator," he says in this book, "is built up of *radioactive* materials which send forth from the instruments an unending stream of powerful ray-charges that penetrate the endocrines and ionize them." Benefits, he stated, included "return to youthful functioning," and successful treatment of such diseases as diabetes, kidney trouble, prostate conditions, tooth decay, arthritis, chronic headache, locomotor ataxia, and obesity.*

A paperback version of Dr. Rubin's book, with his name omitted from the title page, was prepared and used in the Radiendocrinator promotion. The device originally sold for $1,000. The firm later announced that it had been able to "simplify and perfect production methods," and dropped the price to $150.

In 1924 Dr. Rubin was expelled from the membership of the Medical Society of the County of New York and

---

* The theory of the cause and cure of obesity set forth by Dr. Rubin in this book differs from that used to sell Citrophan, cited above. Obesity, he says in the book, "is due largely to faulty thyroid and pituitary gland action. . . . Until the thyroid and pituitary are restored to normal, true obesity can rarely be successfully corrected." The book was copyrighted in 1923 while the Citrophan promotion was active. Dr. Rubin, medical director of Gotham Corporation, apparently held two theories about the cause and cure of obesity simultaneously.

the Medical Society of the State of New York. The Radiendocrinator promotion continued until the early 1930's, when it faded away. In 1936 Dr. Rubin was readmitted to the medical societies.

Another piece of literature is a leaflet issued by the Parker Chiropractic Research Foundation entitled "M.D.'s Comment on Chiropractic." It was one of the items available for quantity purchase by chiropractors at the 1967 Parker seminar that I attended. It is given to patients and to legislators. Copies were sent to members of the Oklahoma State Legislature in 1967 in connection with bills being pushed by chiropractors. Other state and national legislators may receive the leaflet in connection with future activities of the chiropractic lobby, if they have not received it already.

The leaflet contains no fewer than twenty-three statements endorsing chiropractic by persons designated as medical doctors. This is an apparently formidable array, and I have therefore subjected the contents of the leaflet to study. Two of the quotations are from foreign doctors —one English and one French. I did not attempt to check these quotes. An inquiry into the remaining twenty-one turned up a good deal of information.

The American Medical Association's Circulation and Records Department keeps records on every person who graduates from an accredited medical school in the United States, and every person licensed to practice medicine in any of the fifty states of the Union. The information in these records extends back before chiropractic was born. According to these records, only thirteen of the twenty-one "M.D.'s" whose testimonials appear in this leaflet were ever medical doctors.

Of the twenty-one persons, I was able to find some kind of record of eighteen. All of them, including all the M.D.'s, are dead. A nineteenth, if he is not dead, would now be about ninety years old.

I found a definite year of death for seventeen of the testimonial-givers. They all died between ten and fifty years ago. At least five were born before the Civil War, and one was born in 1847, before the end of the Mexican War.

Checking back, I discovered that thirteen of the quotations appear in a booklet entitled *Opinions of Well Known Medical Men and Osteopaths Regarding Chiropractic*, published by the Palmer School of Chiropractic sometime between 1915 and 1920. Five others appear in a booklet of the same title, with no publisher or date indicated, that was probably produced in the early 1930's, and definitely came out before February, 1936, as indicated by a postmark on a copy I have seen (this booklet also contains the thirteen that appear in the 1915–1920 booklet).

Further study of the records of the thirteen genuine M.D.'s revealed an interesting fact. Ten of them were also chiropractors. Their activity dated back to chiropractic's early years, when a small number of medical doctors enlisted under D. D. Palmer's banners. If these ten are representative, M.D.-D.C.'s were mostly men of little standing in the medical world, many of whom were involved in healing superstitions or medical quackery.

One of the M.D.-D.C.'s whose testimonial appears in the Palmer leaflet is Dr. William A. Seeley, the man who was born during the Mexican War. He never graduated from any medical school, but in 1886, in accordance with the usage of the time, he was granted a license by the state of Iowa to practice "homeopathy," a type of herbal medicine. This gave him the right to use the initials M.D. He was an early graduate of the Palmer School and thus became an M.D.-D.C. He died in 1918 at age seventy-one. Half a century later, thanks to the Parker Chiropractic Research Foundation, his testimonial still appears in chiropractic waiting rooms and in the halls of state governments.

Another of the M.D.-chiropractors is Dr. E. W. Feige of Huron, South Dakota. He was born in 1871, graduated from Chicago Homeopathic Medical College in 1895, and was licensed by Iowa in 1895 and by South Dakota in 1897. He subsequently graduated from the Palmer School of Chiropractic. He died in 1936.

In 1910 his name appears as a member of the staff of a group called the Weltmer Institute of Suggestive Therapeutics. A Kansas physician wrote that Feige was reported to be "performing miracles by suggestion."

Later he became much interested in a type of treatment called "aetheronics," involving the use of machines called Streborcam Aetheronic Emanation Instruments. Like the Drown Therapeutic Instruments (see Chapter Five), these machines supposedly cured patients anywhere in the world by transmitting emanations to them. Also like the Drown instruments, aetheronic machines were inspired by the "radionics" theories and devices of Dr. Albert Abrams.

The grand mogul of aetheronics was a man named Dorr Eldred Wood, who set himself up as an "authorized Abrams practitioner," then graduated to aetheronics, which he described as beyond both physics and electronics. Aetheronics machines, says a sales pamphlet, "accomplish desired results, the complete negativing and arresting of disease and toxin activity in the patient regardless of the correctness of the diagnosis." A patient in Japan, the pamphlet states, can be cured in an hour; one in South Africa, in thirty-five minutes; one in Europe, in twenty minutes; "and within a radius of one thousand miles, approximately fifteen minutes are needed to arrest and negative disease and toxin emanations." Prices of the machines ranged from $170 to $450. Feige provided a statement for a booklet of testimonials about the treatment.

A third M.D.-chiropractor whose testimonial appears in the Parker leaflet is Howard L. Cornell, who was born in 1872, graduated from Medico-Chirurgical College of Kansas City in 1902, and was licensed to practice in Missouri and Kansas. In 1917 he graduated from the Palmer School of Chiropractic. He died in 1939.

Cornell's specialty was diagnosis through astrology. An advertisement in the February, 1921, issue of an astrological publication, *The Aquarian Age,* reads:

Cornell wrote an immense work called *The Encyclopedia of Medical Astrology,* offered for sale by Cornell Publishing Company. An ad for the book says, "Seventeen years in writing, this 966-page book on Astro-Diagnosis of every known disease subject is the culmination of Dr. Cornell's life work as a great doctor and astrologer."

Of the three non-chiropractor M.D.'s whose testimonials appear in the leaflet, one is identified as Lee Forest Potter. The same testimonial appears in Thorp McClusky's book *Your Health and Chiropractic,* with the name given as La Forest Potter, and according to AMA records the latter is correct. La Forest Potter was born in 1855 and died in 1951, age ninety-six. He graduated from Boston University School of Medicine in 1884 and was licensed to practice in Massachusetts and New York. He contributed articles to *Physical Culture,* the food faddist magazine run by the late Bernarr MacFadden. He was apparently interested in "cancer cures"; at one time he was associated with a proponent of the so-called "grape juice cure" for cancer, and at another time he was reported to be giving "cancer injections" for $150 each.

The second non-chiropractor M.D. is H. W. Scott. AMA records list Herbert William Scott, who was born in 1867, graduated from the Detroit College of Medicine and Surgery in 1897, and was licensed to practice in Michigan in 1900.

In a promotional booklet issued in 1912 for a contrivance called the Oxypathor, Scott's name appears as recommending and endorsing the machine. The Oxypathor, the booklet says, cures such conditions as appendicitis, diphtheria, blood disorders, catarrh, kidney trouble, heart trouble, gallstones, Bright's disease, blood poisoning, dropsy, pneumonia, typhoid fever, and "most forms of paralysis." "As the dews gather upon the bosom of the sleeping earth to feed and refresh vegetation," the booklet says, "so does the application of the OXYPATHOR, while you rest or sleep, cause your body to increase its vitality and thus overcome its debility in a NATURAL WAY."

Scott moved to Canada in 1912 and died there in 1926.

The third of the non-chiropractor M.D.'s is U. A. Lyle. AMA records list Urban A. Lyle, who was born in 1878, graduated from Physio-Medical College of Indiana in 1903, and was licensed to practice in Indiana in that year. In the late 1920's Lyle was assistant medical director of Indianapolis Cancer Hospital, one of the greatest of all quack cancer promotions. A 1929 bulletin issued by the Indianapolis Better Business Bureau on the hospital calls it "without doubt the most disgraceful institution that has ever been permitted to operate for any length of time in the City of Indianapolis, and one of the worst, if not the worst, in the whole country." The intervening years have done nothing to mellow the verdict.

In form letters sent to prospective customers throughout the country the hospital said, "After years of experience and research, we have found that the best means in combatting this disease, is by the injection (with an ordinary hypodermic syringe) of what we term our Liquid Laboratory Product, this injection being made directly into the cancer, destroying it completely. . . . Usually one treatment (which requires but a few moments' time) destroys the entire cancerous growth."

In its campaign to secure the names of potential customers, the hospital developed a gimmick that may be unique in the annals of medical quackery. It circularized the nation's ministers, offering them a small item such as a fountain pen, a penknife, a pair of cuff links, a watch fob, or a clothes brush, in exchange for the names and addresses of persons known by the minister to be suffering from cancer. The ministers also received certificates good for $25, which sum they would receive as soon as any person whose name they supplied entered the hospital as a patient. The clerics were assured that the cancer victim would never know where the hospital had gotten his or her name.

The hospital's confidence in the venality of some men of the cloth was justified by the results. Names of many cancer sufferers come in from ministers. At hearings before the Indiana State Board of Medical Registration and Examination held in 1929, it was testified that the fountain pens were purchased by the hospital in lots of 600 each and "went in no time."

The hospital then wrote to the people whose names the ministers provided, describing its treatment in glowing terms. Cancer patients poured into Indianapolis from all over the nation. The hospital offered treatment to all types, ranging from terminal cancer victims to people whom subsequent medical examination showed not to have cancer at all. Before treatment began, victims were asked how much money they had, and were required to make advance "down payments" ranging up to $1,000. In desperation, poor people literally handed over their life savings, and rural people mortgaged their farms.

After collecting the advance payment, the hospital kept the patients at $25 a day until their money ran out, and then sent them home. If they inquired about their condition they received curt, angry replies. They were seldom treated or even examined. The license of the hospital's medical director, Dr. Charles C. Root, was later revoked for being intoxicated while in charge of patients and for misrepresenting his ability to cure cancer. The selection of letters from the hospital's victims published in the May 23, 1929, issue of the Indianapolis Better Business Bureau *Bulletin*, in which these and other harrowing circumstances are revealed, was shocking.

The hospital kept the contents of its Liquid Laboratory Product secret. But the Indianapolis Better Business Bureau obtained a sample and had it analyzed. Its principal ingredient was zinc chloride, a common chemical, worthless for treatment of cancer. Thanks in great measure to the bureau's crusade, the hospital closed its doors in June, 1929. Dr. Urban A. Lyle died in 1950, but his endorsement of chiropractic is still being circulated by the Parker Foundation.

As we have noted, eight of the testimonials in the leaflet are by persons claimed by the Parker Foundation to be M.D.'s, but, according to AMA records, they never graduated from an accredited medical school and never held a license. Six of these testimonials appear both in the booklet published by the Palmer School of Chiropractic sometime between 1915 and 1920, and in the booklet of the same name published by an unknown source in the 1930's. The other two appear in the 1930's booklet only.

In these booklets, only four of the eight persons are listed as M.D.'s, and these four are designated as M.D.-chiropractors. The other four are designated as osteopath-chiropractors. The American Osteopathic Association's records confirm that two of them were osteopaths, but the association could find no record of the other two.

Turning first to the four alleged M.D.-chiropractors, all

139

I could find out about one of them, W. E. Brayman, is that he died in Akron, Ohio, in July, 1917.

A second, Edward P. Bailey, was apparently a "naturopath"* who represented himself as an M.D. In the September, 1910, issue of the *Columbus Medical Journal*, a magazine on medical subjects for laymen, he describes "a new treatment for rupture" involving the use of herbs. After his name appear the initials "N.P.D.M." In 1917 he was elected president of the Association of Naturopathic Physicians of California. In the April, 1922, issue of the *Journal* of a group called "The Allied Medical Associations of America" (no relation to the American Medical Association) his name appears with the initials M.D. after it. Bailey died in 1951.

The third person in this group, G. W. Raby, was born in 1873, and ran a drugstore in Hickory, North Carolina. In 1918 he informed the American Medical Association that he was a graduate of Keokuk Medical College, Keokuk, Iowa, Class of 1897. AMA checked but could not find Raby's name in the college's alumni lists.

The fourth person is Frederick L. Fischer, allegedly a physician of Philadelphia, Pennsylvania. His statement, published in the 1915–1920 booklet, is described as having been given at the Second Annual Palmer School of Chiropractic Lyceum at Davenport in 1915. In 1922 the *Journal of the American Medical Association*, commenting on Fischer's testimonial, said, "The records fail to show that any man of this name has any right to call himself 'M.D.' or has ever been licensed to practice medicine; neither does the latest Philadelphia telephone directory show any man in the city of Philadelphia of this name, chiropractor or otherwise."

Of the four osteopath-chiropractors, the American Osteopathic Association has no record of Edward S. Doutt and S. C. Wyatt, both of whose testimonials appeared in the 1915–1920 Palmer School booklet. D. L. Evans, the third man, was a licensed osteopath who graduated from

---

* See footnote p. 21.

Still College of Osteopathy in 1906. He died in 1928. The fourth, J. Franklin Coon, was born in 1854 and was licensed to practice osteopathy in the state of Washington in 1909 at age fifty-five. He died at age seventy-eight in 1932.

Coon had his own pet cure-all. In a half-page ad in the March 13, 1924, issue of the Walla Walla, Washington, *Daily Bulletin,* he attacked the medical profession for ignoring his ideas. He charged M.D.'s with using "DIRTY, CONTEMPTIBLE, DISHONORABLE TRICKS AND DEVICES FOR ATTRACTING AND HOLDING PATIENTS . . . they 'coddle' and intensify disease that their patients may become feeble chronic sufferers; all because they cannot afford to lose the fees such sickness implies."

Further on in the ad he stated: "By them also [the M.D.'s] I am declared a criminal because I have announced to the world that I have been fortunate enough to acquire knowledge of a remedy that enables me to deliver my fellow men from the suffering and ultimate death, to which their unjustifiable methods subject him." This remedy, Coon says, "can cleanse the bloodstream of the pollution that makes possible the development of cancer and tuberculosis." Unfortunately, he continues, he is being required to discontinue advertising his great discovery. He does not specify what the discovery is, either in this ad or in promotional materials for his "Health Institute" in Centralia, Washington, where he allegedly effected numerous cures. But Coon was apparently one of the many chiropractors who were enthusiastic boosters of the theories and machines of Dr. Albert Abrams. A week before his big ad appeared in the Walla Walla paper, a small news item in the Wartsburg, Washington, *Times* noted that Coon had given a public demonstration of the "Abrams Method of Diagnosis" in that town.

These, then, are the men chosen by the Parker Foundation, a leading light in the chiropractic world, to speak for the chiropractor.

Let us now turn to the actual findings of science.

CHAPTER ELEVEN

The Views
of Science

THROUGHOUT THIS BOOK THE AUTHOR HAS QUOTED A NUMber of scientific authorities on various specific aspects of chiropractic theory and practice. These statements, along with other material already set forth, may have amply convinced the reader that there is no scientific basis for chiropractic. Such a reader may skip this chapter, but is advised to keep the book around, and use the chapter later for arguments with friends or with chiropractors. On the other hand, chiropractors, their patients, and persons considering chiropractic treatment, should read on carefully.

There is no known human disease, not even a backache, that is caused by impingement of spinal nerves by subluxations. That is the verdict of science on the Iowa grocer's dream.

The scientific validity of chiropractic theory has been the subject of numerous studies and reports, a few of which will be discussed here.

In 1945 the Medical Society of the State of New York issued a publication entitled *Medicine Men and Men of*

143

Medicine, by Charles M. Bayer. According to this publication, in 1934 the Educational Department of the University of the State of New York addressed a set of four questions to one hundred nationally known specialists in anatomy, bacteriology, orthopedics, pathology, physiology, and roentgenology, whose names were chosen from the publication *American Men of Science.* These were the questions:

(1) In your experience, what "pains and illnesses of the human body" have you found to be caused by a subluxation or misalignment of the spinal vertebrae, other than those caused by trauma?

(2) In your experience, have you ever found the "foramina or apertures between the vertebrae, through which the nerve branches issue from the spinal cord," narrowed and causing pressure upon a nerve or nerves? If so, under what circumstances?

(3) In your judgment, is it possible to reduce a subluxation or misalignment of the vertebrae and thus relieve pressure upon nerve branches "by manipulation of the hand"?

(4) In general, what is your view of chiropractic both as a theory and as an alleged science?

A typical answer to the first question was that of Dr. C. Carl Huber, professor of anatomy and dean of the Graduate School of the University of Michigan: "There is no condition of subluxation or misalignment of the spinal vertebrae in the sense used by the chiropractic practitioner. If such conditions, by reason of accident or disease, actually are found, they require skilled surgery."

Replying to the second question, Dr. R. R. Bensley, Director of the Department of Anatomy of the University of Chicago, said, "In a period of twenty-nine years, during which time I have been Director of this Department, we have never found in our dissecting rooms a single instance in which the foramen or aperture between the vertebrae through which the nerve branches issue from the spinal cord have been so narrowed as to cause pressure upon nerves."

On the third question, Dr. Dean Lewis, surgeon-in-chief of Johns Hopkins Hospital, said, "In my judgment, it is not possible to reduce subluxations or misalignments of the vertebrae and thus relieve pressure of the nerve branches by manipulation of the hand."

On the final question, Dr. Harvey Cushing, then one of the world's leading brain surgeons, wrote, "There is no pathological basis whatever for the theory of chiropractic, and it is silly to allude to it as a science."*

In the late 1940's, at the request of the Subcommittee on Cults of the Medical Society of the State of New York, a three-man commission made a study of chiropractic. Its members were: Dr. Philip B. Armstrong, professor of anatomy, Syracuse University College of Medicine; Dr. Homer D. Keston, associate professor of pathology, Columbia University College of Physicians and Surgeons; and LeRoy L. Barnes, Ph.D., professor of biophysics, Cornell University. The commission's *Report* was published in 1948:

> The fundamental tenet of chiropractic claims that all disease is due primarily to pressure on nerves. It should be emphasized at the very outset that nerve pressure as the primary cause of disease is only a belief. The chiropractors have not demonstrated its truth by scientific experimentation. They have assumed that it is true and, on this assumption, have instituted methods of treatment. There is, however, a large body of scientific fact which conclusively disproves the fundamental tenet of chiropractic.

The *Report* discussed in detail the question of pressure on nerves. It is a fact, says the document, that "pressure on these nerves of sufficient intensity can reduce or abol-

---

* Bayer, *op. cit.*, pp. 36–40.

ish their activity." But it does not follow that chiropractic theory and treatment of disease have any validity.

To begin with, as a simple physical fact, the nerves serving many areas of the body cannot be subject to impingement by vertebrae as they leave the spine, and these nerves are equally beyond the reach of any manual manipulation to relieve the nonexistent impingement.

"Many very important nerves leave the central nervous system through bony openings which are entirely rigid, formed of a solid ring of bone," the *Report* says. "This is true of all the nerves coming from the brain and also the lower spinal nerves. Those from the brain are distributed to all the structures in the face and one of them passes down through the neck and thorax into the abdomen, supplying the heart, lungs, stomach, liver, intestines and other important structures. The lower spinal nerves pass out through the sacrum to the prostate, bladder, uterus, etc. These structures are frequently involved in disease which, according to the chiropractors, is due to pressure on their nerves. No amount of manipulation can change the rigid openings through which these nerves pass from the skull or sacrum."

Nerves serving other important bodily systems do not even pass through the spine, and are therefore equally beyond the chiropractor's reach. "Some of the glands of internal secretion which are so important in regulating various activities of the body are not under the control of the spinal nerves," the *Report* states. This includes the pituitary gland, "the so-called Master Gland of the body."

Again, some tissues have no nerves at all. "The blood is subject to a variety of diseases but receives no nerves, not even in the bones where most of the blood cells are formed. . . . Where do the chiropractors manipulate to relieve a disease existing throughout the body in the blood, a tissue which receives no nerves? Pernicious anemia poses the same problem."

Other facts call into serious question the chiropractic premise that impaired nerve function somehow renders the areas of the body served by such nerves susceptible to disease. For example, skin areas with impaired or severed nerve function are not more susceptible to cancer. Again, many human maladies are helped, not aggravated, by the severing of nerves. "A number of nerve-cutting operations have been devised for the relief of a variety of conditions. . . . Here we see that some disease conditions are relieved by abolishing nerve function which is diametrically opposed to fundamental chiropractic belief."

In 1963 a bill was introduced in the Quebec Legislature to license chiropractors and permit the practice of chiropractic in Quebec. A Royal Commission on Chiropractic was set up to collect information and make a report to the legislature. The commission, in turn, sought and received presentations from interested parties. The Quebec College of Physicians and Surgeons submitted the 64-page *Brief* to which we have referred in previous chapters.

The *Brief* noted the apparent complete indifference of chiropractic to the question of whether its doctrine is true. In common with everyone else who propounds a scientific theory, says the *Brief*, chiropractors have the "duty" and the "responsibility" of submitting their theories "to at least the minimum exigencies of scientific proof" before applying them wholesale to matters involving health, sickness, life, and death. "Chiropractors have had every scientific method available to them," the *Brief* states. "Sixty-eight years constitute a sufficient period for the experimental proof of a limited number of facts." But chiropractors have never shown the slightest interest in experimental proof. Their posture is made all the more dubious by the fact that highly sophisticated means for conducting decisive experiments on their fundamental premises lie readily to hand.

Thus, the chiropractor claims that nervous impulses are in some way disturbed or impaired by spinal subluxations. The obvious medical question is, what kind of disturbance? "No chiropractor has ever defined, either quantitatively or qualitatively, what chiropractic means

147

by perturbation of nervous impulse," the *Brief* states. "Is it their number, their amplitude, their frequency, the speed of their propagation, or their wave patterns which are affected? All of these qualities can be identified, recorded, and studied. . . . Exceptionally sensitive apparatus is available to anyone wishing to use it."

Again, chiropractors claim that these impairments of nervous impulse cause disease. "By what experimental proof have they demonstrated a causative relationship between disturbance of nervous flow and the development of illnesses which they claim to cure? Here, again, absolutely none."

This indifference to scientific experiment contrasts sharply with chiropractic's enthusiasm for merchandising itself. "It is indeed astonishing," says the *Brief,* "that there has been such a lack of effort, or of concern for scientific truth, especially if one considers the effort that has gone into selling the theory to the general public—when the world to be convinced was the scientific world. Let the theory gain acceptance in the world of scholars, and all the troubles of the chiropractor will vanish."

The affidavits made by professors and medical experts in connection with the Jerry R. England case in Louisiana in 1965 provide a wealth of scientific information on chiropractic.

Subluxations are discussed by Dr. Irvin Cahen, professor and head of the orthopedic department at Louisiana State University School of Medicine. A subluxation, he says, "involves an alteration of the normally opposed surfaces of a joint," as opposed to a luxation or dislocation, "in which the joint surfaces are completely separated." Subluxations, so defined, occur all the time in normal motion.

There is also such a thing as a "fixed subluxation," in which the surfaces do not return to normal opposition after movement. These "result only from pathology involving capsular or ligamental tears or alteration in the actual bony structure." Whether subluxations be those of normal movement, or fixed, they cannot and do not impinge on nerves. "It is my knowledge," he says, "that in chiropractic considerations the joints that are considered to be subluxed are those which we term facets, situated to the sides of the major body articulations. These joints cannot impinge upon a nerve root without major displacement."

There *is* such a thing as a pinched nerve, he says, resulting from such problems as a ruptured disc, displaced bone fragments, or tumefaction, but "in no instance has there been any scientific evidence that manipulation of a subluxed joint will correct these abnormalities." He also agrees with his fellow scientists that "the premise that an irritated nerve resulting from compression at an area is responsible for a disease has no scientific basis."

Dr. Cahen and Dr. Solomon D. Winokur both stressed the dangers arising from the incomplete patterns of both diagnosis and treatment that are inherent in chiropractic theory and practice. This is true even for the treatment of back pains and spinal problems, to say nothing of the complete range of ills that chiropractors treat. "In order to be able to properly manipulate any area of the spine," says Dr. Winokur, "it is first necessary and most important to make an accurate diagnosis. In order to make an accurate diagnosis it is essential that the person attempting to make such a diagnosis have a complete background in all of the normal and pathological conditions related to or around the vertebral structure." So-called back pains, he pointed out, can be most deceptive. "For example, there are many times where a back pain is being produced as a result of a prostatitis, acute appendix, acute gall bladder condition, and female disorders, tubal or ovarian, or retroverted uterus which produces low-back pain. Without a proper understanding of the surgical implication of these things a proper diagnosis is impossible."

Dr. Alton Ochsner, Sr., for thirty-one years chairman of the department and professor of surgery at Tulane University School of Medicine and now professor emeritus at Tulane, firmly denied in his affidavit the chiropractor's central belief that subluxations other than displacements due to normal movement are a prevalent or omnipresent phenomenon. He also stated that the chiropractor's claim to be able to feel subluxations comes close to being a physical impossibility: "Furthermore, it is almost impossible, and I think impossible, to feel any subluxation of any part of the spine below the cervical region because of the large mass of muscle overlying the vertebrae which makes it impossible for anyone to feel it."

Dr. George Nelson Ronstrom, professor of anatomy at Louisiana State University School of Medicine, bore down on another aspect of the matter that is by now familiar to the reader. "Anatomically," he said, "we find that forty-three pairs of nerve trunks carry the flow from the brain and spinal cord to various body structures or organs. However, the anatomist finds that only twenty-six pairs of spinal nerves are available to spinal manipulation. The brain and spinal cord from which the nerves originate, twelve pairs of cranial nerves, and five pairs of sacral nerves, simply are not available to manipulation because they pass through orifices made up of fused and immovable bones, and are therefore inaccessible to chiropractic manipulation." The inaccessible nerves include "various nerve supplies to the head, senses of smell, taste, hearing and sight, organs of the neck, respiratory apparatus, heart, stomach, small intestine, part of large intestine, pancreas, gall bladder, liver, spleen, kidneys, pelvic organs and part of lower limbs." Dr. Ronstrom then quietly asks a blockbuster question. "This anatomical fact immediately raises the following question in the scientific mind: Why should the twenty-six pairs of spinal nerves accessible to spinal manipulation have such a great importance and the rest so little?"

Several of the experts had taken the time to read chiropractic writings and textbooks in the areas of their specialties. They found the books full of error and untruth. What impressed the experts is the way in which the chiropractic writers ignored whole mountains of material findings and evidence that have been produced by the vast labors of twentieth-century science.*

Dr. Andrew V. Friedrichs, assistant professor of pathology and bacteriology at Tulane, reacted with incredulity to a pamphlet called "The Chiropractor Looks at Infection," by J. R. Verner and C. W. Weiant.** "To put it bluntly," Dr. Friedrichs says, "the chiropractors advocate in this pamphlet that all immunization and inoculation for polio, tetanus, typhoid, smallpox, diphtheria, to name a few, and many other diseases which are combatted by immunization and inoculation, be discarded, to be replaced by manipulation of the spinal column, to normalize the flow of nerve impulses. . . . The authors advocate manipulation following trauma, where a fracture is present. Manipulation is the answer in acute infections, where an abscess has formed, or an acute appendix. Surgical procedures are completely ruled out." Dr. Friedrichs obviously had trouble believing what he was reading, and noted that the authors "even attempt to prove that their ridiculous conclusions are correct." To Dr. Friedrichs, the pamphlet was "amusing" and "ludicrous."

Dr. Richard M. Paddison discussed in detail some sections of *The Chiropractic Physician's Manual*, by O. V. Allers, a faculty member of Lincoln Chiropractic College, that related to Dr. Paddison's specialty of neurology. On

---

* Actually, this is probably easily explained. Modern medical knowledge demonstrates that chiropractic theory is false, and the chiropractor begins with the assumption that it is true. He must therefore necessarily discount or ignore whole areas of modern science and research. "The principles of chiropractic are just as sound today as when they were first promulgated in 1895," says Mortimer Levine, D.C., chairman of the department of chiropractic at the Chiropractic Institute of New York, in his book *The Structural Approach to Chiropractic* (Comet Press, 1964). In his preface to this book C. W. Weiant, dean emeritus of the Chiropractic Institute of New York, calls Dr. Levine "one of the truly great intellects of chiropractic history."

** For discussion of another work by these authors, see Chapter Six.

the subject of migraine headache, "the manual points out that the cause is unknown, which is not true." The book of course specifies chiropractic adjustments for treatment. "Such a concept denies the scientific data which have been accumulated so painstakingly and are well documented in the medical literature."

The *Manual* also recommends adjustments of subluxations for peripheral neuritis. Among other things, says Dr. Paddison, "there are peripheral neuropathies which affect the cranial nerves, which cannot be involved in subluxation." A theory that specifies subluxations as the cause of this malady "is a complete denial of what is known by modern medicine in terms of peripheral nerve function and diseases."

On polio, the *Manual* refers to a book called *Taking the Terror Out of Polio* by a Dr. Dunn, and recommends the treatment set forth in that book. It includes, says Dr. Paddison, "isolation of the patient, alternation of water and orange juice diet, general and specific adjustments, relaxing the muscles of the back with knifelike thrust correction of the paralysis of the neck, release of the spasm of the scapula by way of deep goading bilateral manipulation of the inguinal glands, release of the interosseus membranes in the legs, foot adjustments and manipulations of the abdominal viscera." Dr. Paddison reviews current scientific knowledge of this disease, and deals with the material in the *Manual* curtly: "The use of manipulative therapy in this disorder can only be condemned as 'quackery.'"

On epilepsy, the *Manual* says that there are many theories regarding the etiologies of the disease "which you should forget immediately." Brain damage during birth, injuries in childhood, and tumorous growths, the *Manual* says, are among the etiological theories that have never been proven. "These statements," says Dr. Paddison, "constitute a bold-faced prevarication of the available scientific data which have been accumulated in the past thirty-five years regarding epilepsy or convulsive disorders."

The *Manual* states that subluxations in the cervical and upper dorsal spine are commonly found in epileptic patients. "There is not a shred of scientific data in terms of the modern concept of epilepsy which allows us to even consider spinal subluxations and their adjustment in the causation of seizure states." Calling the information in the *Manual* "sheer and wanton quackery," Dr. Paddison goes on to say, "Patients are duped, misled and have their diagnosis and treatment either interfered with or delayed to the point of personal hazard because some seizure states can lead to what we call status epilepticus, a grave medical disorder which may lead to death or serious mental disability of a permanent nature."

The views of modern science on chiropractic are reflected in HEW's 1968 Report, which recommended against the inclusion of chiropractors in the Medicare program. "There is a body of basic scientific knowledge related to health, disease, and health care," the Report says. "Chiropractic practitioners ignore or take exception to much of this knowledge despite the fact that they have not undertaken adequate scientific research. . . . Chiropractic theory and practice are not based upon the body of basic knowledge related to health, disease, and health care that has been widely accepted by the scientific community."*

In the face of this overwhelming scientific testimony, what is one to make of the fact that many persons report that they feel better after being treated by a chiropractor?** In some instances this may reflect psychological factors, as noted by Dr. Richard M. Paddison, or the self-limiting nature of most symptoms, as described by Dr. Milton Helpern and Dr. Robert W. Buck, in the preceding chapter.

In his England case affidavit, Dr. Cahen discusses the relief from back complaints that some patients report after receiving chiropractic manipulations. "I would consider

---

* HEW Report, pp. 196–97.
** Others, of course, report feeling worse.

this temporary relief is entirely due to the application of heat or the massage of musculature or the stretching of sore muscles in the same overall concept that we apply physical therapy to the body as an adjunct to rehabilitation. I do not believe that such temporary relief is other than the effect of heat and massage."

Suggestive comment appears in HEW's Report. "The chiropractor attempts to move the vertebra with his hands so that it will not interfere with nerve function," says the Report. "It may be that the chiropractor, in this maneuver, is not affecting nerve function but actually is restoring the normal mobility of the joint. In this manner, the chiropractor may in many cases relieve pain and loss of function with the spinal adjustment. Referred pain to other parts of the body from joint dysfunction may be mistaken for a disease process, and when the spinal adjustment relieves the pain, this may be thought to be a cure of the 'disease.'" In its conclusions, the Report says, "Manipulation [including chiropractic manipulation] may be a valuable technique for relief of pain due to loss of mobility of joints. Research in this area is inadequate; therefore, it is suggested that research that is based upon the scientific method be undertaken with respect to manipulation."*

The Report makes two things clear. First, such research was not reflected in the materials submitted by chiropractic associations to the HEW study group in support of the alleged scientific validity of chiropractic. "The little research that is done [by chiropractors]," says the Report, "seems to be directed at proving that D. D. Palmer's teachings were right, rather than taking an objective look at all possible causes of disease."** Second, if patients receive any benefit from chiropractic treatment, the benefits do not arise from the chiropractic theory. Chiropractors, the Report states, "believe that the subluxation is the most significant causal factor in disease, because they feel that it interferes with normal nerve function. However, no evi-

* HEW Report, pp. 157, 197.
** P. 181.

dence has been found in the literature, nor has any information been submitted to this study, to prove that a subluxation, if it exists, is a cause of disease."*

It hardly seems necessary to go on. The substance of the matter has been summarized in a statement on chiropractic issued by the McGill University faculty of medicine in 1963. "The theory which underlies chiropractic is false," the McGill faculty says. "Biology is probably the most complex and difficult of sciences and human biology its most important branch. To reduce it to one primary mechanical concept is simpleminded and dangerous." It is hard for the author of this book to imagine how any intelligent person, and even any intelligent chiropractor, could really believe otherwise.

---

* P. 156.

CHAPTER TWELVE

Toward a Solution

"THERE WAS CONSIDERABLE PRESSURE FROM CHIROPRACTORS and their patients for the inclusion of their services under Title 18 [of the Medicare Act] this year. I dislike intensely being in a position between two professional groups [medical doctors and chiropractors] requiring me as a layman to evaluate the relative merits of their services. If chiropractors should not be practicing the healing arts, the remedy is to stop the state from licensing them or to insist on an upgrading of the profession to the point where the public will not be threatened."

A member of the U.S. House of Representatives made these comments in correspondence with one of his constituents in 1967. They provide some insights into how chiropractic achieved its status as the only legally recognized and licensed medical superstition in the United States. They also place ultimate responsibility for both the problem and its solution where it properly belongs—on the doorsteps of the state legislatures.

The public cannot be blamed for not realizing that chiropractic has no scientific foundation. This is the legislatures' fault. People should be able to assume, and obviously do assume, that a state-licensed "doctor" is practicing a valid healing art.

This feeling is reinforced by the general public awareness that substantial provisions for safety and scientific accuracy surround other areas of health care. In the field of drugs, for example, Congress has enacted legislation prohibiting the use of any new drugs on human beings until both their safety and their efficacy have been established in a series of highly scientific procedures, involving continuous tests and complex safeguards. Laws of this kind represent an alliance between science and legislation to protect the public. By contrast, chiropractic licensing acts bring science and politics into direct conflict. Chiropractors have had great success in confusing this issue by representing their differences with medicine as being a scientific controversy between "two professional groups" instead of what it really is—a conflict between science and a scientific fairy tale.

From its infancy chiropractic looked to politics and licensing, not as a way of working with science but as a protection against science. An important factor in chiropractic's present position is that it succeeded in getting licensure laws through thirty-two of the nation's forty-eight rurally dominated state legislatures by the year 1925, almost before the modern era of health care and health legislation began. From then on, with a comfortable majority of states granting recognition and use of the title "doctor," chiropractors conducted intensive campaigns to reduce the remaining legislatures one by one. Today all states except Louisiana and Mississippi have passed laws licensing chiropractors. In some instances the laws were passed after years of ceaseless activity by chiropractic groups. The last two holdout states are being kept under heavy siege, of which the Jerry R. England case in Louisiana was a characteristic feature.

From the early 1920's on, legislators who were aware of the conflict between chiropractic and science felt that they were in a dilemma because so many states had already licensed chiropractors. A possible way out, they thought, was to vote for the license law, which would at least give the state the power to control and limit chiropractic practice. This attitude was cultivated by chiropractors, who joined the side of the angels by noting that they had come voluntarily to the legislature to seek an act which would permit the state to oversee their activities. Chiropractic licensing acts thus secured the votes not only of legislators who were acting as vote brokers, but of some more civic-minded ones who thought that it might be the best way to deal with an anomalous situation.

The truth, of course, is that the limitations placed on the scope of their practice by the state laws are of little moment to chiropractors compared to the granting of the state's "doctor's" license.

Even the best-intentioned provisions of the best state laws bring about perverted results. The requirement that chiropractic aspirants pass state-sponsored basic science exams does not qualify chiropractors to treat the sick. What it *has* done is to arm chiropractic schools with a shiny new rationale for existence, and a shiny new hunting license to prey on innocent persons, many of them with limited educational backgrounds, who are seeking a career. They prepare these people to pass the exams. While doing so they give them a limited education, and inculcate a false theory.

The most important limitations posed on chiropractic by the licensing laws prohibit chiropractors from prescribing drugs or performing surgery. This does not grieve chiropractors. A licensing act was not necessary to place these prohibitions on chiropractors in the first place, since existing medical practice acts exclude all non-doctors from these activities. Moreover, it is a "limitation" with which the chiropractor lives easily. "It is apparent," says the HEW Report, "that state licensing laws do not restrict the scope of chiropractic practice since they do not infringe upon chiropractic philosophy or approach to health and disease. A practitioner operating under the

159

chiropractic philosophy has no interest in the use of major surgery or drugs and therefore a prohibition against these treatments does not alter his mode of practice."

The Parker seminar *Textbook* contains a number of comments for the chiropractor to make to his patients to undermine their belief in medical drugs, for example:

"Health cannot be found in a bottle, Mrs. Jones."

"Chiropractic searches for, and removes, causes of diseases, Mrs. Jones, rather than treats effects. That is why chiropractic has been successful, many times after all other methods of healing have failed."

In 1963 chiropractors succeeded in getting a licensure law through the New York State Legislature after a fifty-year struggle. In the steps leading to the passage of the act a familiar scene was enacted. The bill was introduced, sent to committee, and hearings were held. Scientists testified that chiropractic theory is false and that its practice is a public health hazard.

The pressure on well-intentioned legislators to vote for licensure anyway because it would allow the state to oversee chiropractic was discussed by Dr. Milton Helpern, Chief Medical Examiner of the City of New York. "The argument that, by licensure, more effective control would be obtained over the activities of chiropractors is specious and fallacious," Dr. Helpern said. "It serves some good and is practicable to license podiatrists, whose work is well defined and activities limited by definition, and the public is protected by the limitations and hygiene supervision that such licensure provides; but podiatrists do not practice on the basis of any spurious theory like that of spinal nerve impingements."

Many of the witnesses were obviously mystified that such legislation could be the subject of serious consideration in modern America. A joint statement prepared by Dr. Frank W. McKee, associate dean of the University of Rochester School of Medicine and Dentistry; Dr. Charles H. Saunders, associate dean of Cornell University School of Medicine; Dr. Marcus D. Kogel, dean of the Albert Einstein College of Medicine; and Dr. Ralph

E. Snyder, then president and dean of New York Medical College, said, "It is an incredible anachronism that in an age when this nation leads the world in many areas of scientific endeavor, New York State should be asked to place its seal of approval on a group of persons claiming to be practitioners who are largely ignorant of the accepted and proven science of health and disease."

The legislators listened gravely to this and other scientific testimony. They then went back into private session and reported the bill out favorably. The legislature passed it, and Governor Rockefeller signed it.*

Such scenes, enacted for decades in state houses throughout the country, make it obvious that scientists and chiropractors are communicating with legislators on different wavelengths, and the chiropractors are on the one that counts. Scientists come to legislative hearings armed with information, and chiropractors come armed with votes.

The tactics by which the chiropractic lobby achieves its victories are now being displayed in campaigns to have chiropractic treatment covered under federal Medicare and state-sponsored Medicaid programs. The key to their

---

* The chiropractic licensing laws of many states have "grandfather clauses"; that is, chiropractors already in practice when the law was passed were not required to meet its educational requirements or to take prescribed tests. Under these provisions, substantial numbers of chiropractors have been admitted to practice who have little or no education of any kind and got their "doctor's degrees" from fly-by-night diploma mills. New York State's law did not contain a grandfather clause and required chiropractors to take examinations in order to get their licenses. Chiropractors, who had fought so long for the law, promptly waged another campaign to avoid its examination requirements. They first challenged the constitutionality of requiring such exams. When this suit failed, almost 1,800 chiropractors showed up to take the examination in April, 1964, but they then filed another suit to prevent the state from grading the exams. This suit, too, was unsuccessful, and a compilation of the grades showed that more than a thousand had failed, including chiropractors who had been treating the sick for many years.

success is the recruitment of friends, allies, and supporters at the community level.

In their successful campaign in 1967 to be included in New York State's Medicaid program, they secured remarkably large amounts of coverage in the daily and weekly newspapers of smaller cities and towns. A typical headline was that for a story in the Nyack, New York, *Journal News:*

CHIROPRACTORS UNDER MEDICARE?

LOCAL DOCTOR
HEADS DRIVE
FOR PASSAGE

The local "doctor" was, of course, a chiropractor.

Some of these stories got fifteen to twenty inches of news space, far more than could be accounted for by the newspaper's occasional need for small filler material. They were, in many instances, the fruit of years of friendly cultivation of the local press.

The letters-to-the-editor columns of these papers were also flooded by letters praising chiropractic and urging its inclusion under Medicaid. Some of the letters were signed by chiropractors. Others appeared under such signatures as "Friend of the Chiropractors," and "Satisfied Chiropractic Patient." Little of this intensive coverage was answered by the scientific community.

In a "Meet Your Friendly Chiropractor" campaign, chiropractors conducted old-fashioned community gatherings in local schools and churches, providing free hot dogs, cotton candy, and soda pop. Themes of these gatherings included:

"Come learn the truth about chiropractic. Learn why AMA is fighting us."

"Find out for yourself about the plot by organized medicine to thwart the greatest medical treatment of the age. Come one, come all!"

At these gatherings chiropractors offered free medical

or health checkups and a free "posture analysis." It is a safe bet that they found many a subluxation in urgent need of chiropractic adjustment. Free chiropractic treatment was offered to children under twelve, along with reduced rates for senior citizens, and money-back guarantees for all comers who accepted treatment.

Chiropractors have long been involved in campaigns among their own confreres to become highly active in local affairs and civic activities, such as PTA's, Boy Scout troops, and church groups. They even volunteer to serve as "team health officers" for Little League baseball teams. When the time comes to secure community help for such measures as chiropractic licensing or chiropractic inclusion under Medicaid, they are already well placed.

In the New York Medicaid campaign they approached community leaders, especially ministers, and collected reams of signed statements from these persons urging the legislature to look on the chiropractors' request favorably. In a supplementary activity, chiropractors conducted an intensive petition campaign among their patients and community friends. By March, 1967, when a bill to place chiropractic care under Medicaid was introduced in the state legislature, the chiropractors already had over 100,000 signatures.

The legislators went into executive session on the matter and decided that a bill wasn't even necessary; the matter could be quietly handled by the State Department of Health. On July 31st the state health department mailed letters to chiropractors informing them that they were included in the Medicaid program, and providing them with information on standards and fees. There was no public announcement.

The major weapon used by chiropractors to avoid discussion of the scientific validity of chiropractic is to charge that anyone doubting or attacking chiropractic is, *prima facie,* part of a vaguely defined "organized medical monopoly" or "medical conspiracy." Every medical person, from local physicians who speak out in opposition to chiropractic at the community level, to deans of the nation's medical schools and heads of research laboratories who testify at state and federal hearings, is tarred with the same brush.

In all this intensive and amazingly skillful political campaigning, state and county chiropractic groups receive expert help and strong back-up from the two national chiropractic associations. Much of the program of these two groups is oriented toward political action, and the activities are guided by political veterans who have both the experience and the contacts. The executive director of the American Chiropractic Association, the larger of the two groups, is Norman A. Erbe, former governor of Iowa.

While carrying out these activities, chiropractors have been able to prevent unfavorable publicity from appearing in the nation's press by establishing a reputation for being litigious. Recently a leading science writer was commissioned by a major national magazine to do a research piece on chiropractic. He submitted the piece and the magazine accepted it. In one of its issues the magazine noted that the piece would appear in a near-future issue. A chiropractic group contacted the magazine, and received affirmation that the article would be unfriendly to chiropractic. A spokesman for the group told the magazine that if the piece were published, large numbers of chiropractors would file individual libel suits against the publication, charging that they had been professionally damaged. The magazine's lawyers, who had gone over the piece with great care, were confident that such actions could be successfully defended. But the magazine decided that the whole project was not worth the many thousands of dollars that such defense would require. It paid the writer in full, and never ran the article.

At this writing, chiropractors are involved in a series of aggressive new legislative campaigns, some of them involving state legislation, and others representing bold new efforts to secure equality and parity with the medical profession in broad areas of national health care. A partial list of these tireless activities of the chiropractic lobby appears in Appendix C of this book. If decisive measures are not taken, there is every reason to believe that these new efforts to make chiropractic a central feature of health care in the United States will succeed. "Do not expect any senator to oppose chiropractic on the floor of the Senate," a U.S. senator told a Louisiana physician in 1967. "There is too much voter support."

It is of course obvious that the U.S. representative whose comments to a constituent are cited at the beginning of this chapter put his finger on the nub of the problem—the official licensing of chiropractors by the states. From this initial misstep everything else follows. His suggestion that chiropractic could perhaps be "upgraded" to conform with science is one for which there is little practical hope, since the central, unifying belief of chiropractic theory is false. To "upgrade" chiropractic would require the elimination of this theory—and that would mean the elimination of chiropractic.

Whatever the difficulties involved, state legislatures can no longer ignore their public obligation to face the issues and the facts, to acknowledge their error, and to set things straight. First of all, legislation in scientific fields that pays no attention to science is bad law, and shows a deep failure on the part of legislators to fulfill their responsibility to their constituents. Second, in this country at this time, anyone claiming to have a valid treatment for human illness should be required to show its validity before the bar of science before receiving a state license to use it on the sick. Third, the correct way to deal with treatment methods that cannot or will not submit to the judgment of scientific research is not to limit and oversee them, but to prohibit them. By abandoning all these precepts in the face of the political pressures created by chiropractors, state legislatures have created a state-supported medical superstition.

Nothing is to be gained, and a great deal—including human lives—will be lost by further postponing action on the problem. The theory of chiropractic is scientifically false, and treatments given in accordance with the

165

theory bear no relationship to the cause or cure of human disease. Its practice should therefore be prohibited, and its personnel should be retrained to enter other professions.

The first step, and one that must be taken immediately, is to prohibit further use of X ray by chiropractors. The dangers of X ray are so manifest that its use in the pursuit of any invalid or irrational healing procedure should be strictly against the law. In permitting chiropractic X ray, legislators have failed their responsibility to the public in a most serious way.

The next step is for each state to create an orderly program for withdrawing chiropractic licenses. As part of this program, consultations should be held between state legislators and the scientific community to discover where needs exist for persons in physiotherapy, physical rehabilitation, and other areas which make use of paramedical personnel. People are badly needed in many of these fields. Chiropractors should then be consulted, and those wishing to remain in the field of health should be offered full retraining in order to pursue skilled careers in one or another of these areas, where their activities will promote scientific progress and serve important public needs. Chiropractors wishing to leave the field of health entirely should have available to them special assistance—a "chiropractor's GI bill"—for reschooling and retraining in any other field that they might wish to enter.

Such a program is the least that the states can do in view of the central responsibility that they bear toward both chiropractors and the public for creating the current situation. It should never have happened in the first place. When public servants, some misguided and some cynical, fail in their responsibilities, there is always a price to pay.

A guiding principle for state action is provided by the Jerry R. England case. As the reader will remember, England and other chiropractors sued the Louisiana State Board of Medical Examiners, to try to force the board to permit chiropractors to practice in Louisiana. Louisiana and Mississippi are the only states in the Union that refuse to license chiropractors.

In 1965 a three-judge Federal District Court for the Eastern District of Louisiana ruled against the chiropractors. The chiropractors appealed to the Supreme Court, but the Supreme Court affirmed the District Court's ruling in July, 1966.

The essence of the District Court's position is simple, and it seems remarkable that it has been lost sight of in the chiropractic controversy. The state, said the District Court, has a right to insist on uniform educational and scientific standards for entering the healing arts. This test, which is an elementary one, is nevertheless one that chiropractic cannot meet because its beliefs and practice are scientifically false. While all but one of its sister states succumbed to the political skills of the chiropractic lobby, Louisiana, its legislature, and its public health officials have stubbornly and steadfastly pointed out that the Emperor has no clothes.

The only proper course that other states can take is to follow Louisiana's precept that health care laws should accord with science. This inescapably means the end of the Iowa grocer's dream.

Appendices

Chiropractors and Medicare

The Department of Health, Education and Welfare's Report entitled *Independent Practitioners Under Medicare* is described on pages 20–22.

The members of the eight-man expert review panel on chiropractic and naturopathy were:

Donald Duncan, M.A., Ph.D., Chairman, Professor and Chairman of Department of Anatomy, University of Texas Medical Branch, Galveston, Texas.

Jack Edeiken, M.D., Department of Radiology, Jefferson Medical College Hospital, Philadelphia, Pennsylvania.

James J. Feffer, M.D., Associate Dean of Clinical Affairs, George Washington University Medical Center, Washington, D. C.

James D. Hardy, Ph.D., D.Sc., Director, John B. Pierce Foundation of Connecticut, Inc., New Haven, Connecticut.

John McMillan Mennell, M.D., Chief, Physical Medicine and Rehabilitation, Philadelphia General Hospital, Philadelphia, Pennsylvania.

Joseph E. Milgrim, M.D., Professor of Clinical Orthopaedic Surgery, Albert Einstein College of Medicine, New York, New York.

Bernard Sandler, M.D., Director, Rehabilitation Medicine, Kingsbrook Jewish Medical Center, Brooklyn, New York.

Walter I. Wardwell, Ph.D., Professor of Sociology, Department of Sociology, University of Connecticut, Storrs, Connecticut.

The Report's conclusions and recommendations, which appear on pages 196–97, are reprinted in full below.

Conclusions and Recommendations

1. There is a body of basic scientific knowledge related to health, disease, and health care. Chiropractic practitioners ignore or take exception to much of this knowledge despite the fact that they have not undertaken adequate scientific research.

2. There is no valid evidence that subluxation, if it exists, is a significant factor in disease processes. Therefore, the broad application to health care of a diagnostic procedure such as spinal analysis and a treatment procedure such as spinal adjustment is not justified.

3. The inadequacies of chiropractic education, coupled with a theory that de-emphasizes proven causative factors in disease processes, proven methods of treatment, and differential diagnosis, make it unlikely that a chiropractor can make an adequate diagnosis and know the appropriate treatment, and subsequently provide the indicated treatment or refer the patient. Lack of these capabilities in independent practitioners is undesirable because: appropriate treatment could be delayed or prevented entirely; appropriate treatment might be interrupted or stopped completely; the treatment offered could be contraindicated; all treatments have some risk involved with

their administration, and inappropriate treatment exposes the patient to this risk unnecessarily.

4. Manipulation (including chiropractic manipulation) may be a valuable technique for relief of pain due to loss of mobility in joints. Research in this area is inadequate; therefore, it is suggested that research based upon the scientific method be undertaken with respect to manipulation.

Recommendation

Chiropractic theory and practice are not based upon the body of basic knowledge related to health, disease, and health care that has been widely accepted by the scientific community. Moreover, irrespective of its theory, the scope and quality of chiropractic education do not prepare the practitioner to make an adequate diagnosis and provide appropriate treatment. Therefore, it is recommended that chiropractic service not be covered in the Medicare program.

Chiropractic Colleges in the U.S.

COLLEGES ACCREDITED BY THE AMERICAN CHIROPRACTIC ASSOCIATION * ("MIXERS")

Chiropractic Institute of New York
New York City

Columbia Institute of Chiropractic
New York City

Lincoln College of Chiropractic
Indianapolis, Indiana

Logan College of Chiropractic
St. Louis, Missouri

* ACA *Journal of Chiropractic,* October, 1968, p. 24. An "Editor's Note" appended to the list reads, "Since July 5, 1968, the Chiropractic Institute of New York has been affiliated with the National College of Chiropractic." The HEW Report lists an additional institution, Western States Chiropractic College, Portland, Oregon, as being "affiliated with ACA; not accredited" (p. 306).

Los Angeles College of Chiropractic
Los Angeles, California

National College of Chiropractic
Lombard, Illinois

Northwestern College of Chiropractic
Minneapolis, Minnesota

Texas Chiropractic College
Pasadena, Texas

COLLEGES RECOGNIZED BY INTERNATIONAL CHIROPRACTORS ASSOCIATION ("STRAIGHTS") *

Cleveland College of Chiropractic
Kansas City, Missouri

Cleveland College of Chiropractic
Los Angeles, California

Palmer College of Chiropractic
Davenport, Iowa

---

* Undated leaflet entitled *Loans, Grants and Scholarships* published by the association. According to the HEW Report, Columbia Institute of Chiropractic is accredited by both associations.

The Chiropractic Lobby at Work

A Partial List of Recent Chiropractic Legislation Introduced in Various States

Amendment of Restrictive Provisions on the Use of X Rays—(N. Y.)

Chiropractic Coverage under Workman's Compensation Laws—(Ky., N. Y.)

Chiropractic Coverage under Various Types of Insurance Provisions—(Md., N. Y., Okla.)

Introduction of New Licensure Laws—(La., Mass., Miss.)

Broadening the Definition and Scope of Practice of Chiropractic—(Mich., N. C., Pa.)

Chiropractors as Coroners—(Minn.)

Service in Armed Forces to Act as Equivalent to the Practice of Chiropractic for Licensure Eligibility—(N. Y.)

177

Special Exemption from Jury Duty for Chiropractors—(N. Y.)

Qualification of Chiropractors to Give Physical Examinations for Marriage Licenses—(N. Y.)

Chiropractic Coverage under Medical Service Plans—(R. I.)

Chiropractic Coverage under Welfare Programs and Medical Aid to the Aged—(Vt.)

Chiropractors as Competent Expert Witnesses in Personal Injury Actions—(W. Va.)

Eliminating Postgraduate and Refresher Course Requirements—(N. J.)

Establishing a Separate Board of Chiropractic Examiners—(W. Va., Wash.)

Allowing Chiropractors the Use of the Titles "Doctor" or "Physician"—(Fla., Wis., N. D., Wash.)

"Straight" Bill—Adjustment by Hands Only—(Ill.)

Recognition of National Board of Chiropractic Examiners—(Ala., Conn., N. D.)

Outpatient Treatment in Hospitals for Indigent—(Fla., Ky.)

Use of State Laboratories Facilities—(Fla.)

Establishment of Scholarships for the Study of Chiropractic—(Fla.)

Two-Year College Pre-Professional Requirement—Delayed Effect—(Ill.)

Allowing the Use of Diet and Nutritional Supplements—(Iowa)

Removal of Certain Science Requirements (Physics, Chemistry, and Biology) in Pre-Professional Curriculum Requirements—(Md.)

Exempting Chiropractors from Provision in Illinois Law Which Prohibits Those Persons Who Took Written Examination and Failed from Becoming Licensed without Examination—(Ill.)

Chiropractic Coverage under Title XIX of Medicare—(Mich.)

Protect yourself and your family!

Don't be one of the "taken"!

BUYER, BEWARE. Each time you walk into a store, call a serviceman, or sign a contract, you run the risk of being "taken." And not just by fly-by-night operators either. Some of the best-known and respected companies in the country lend their names to unscrupulous practices.

● Now, Sidney Margolius, leading consumer authority and an expert in financial management, shows you how to avoid being "tricked" by shady operators and operations. In his book, *The Innocent Consumer vs. The Exploiters,* you'll discover:

● How you can save up to 90 per cent on your drug bills without changing stores. (See page 195)

● The simple "instant" process that lets you calculate the real interest on a loan. (See page 37)

● Why your department store is so anxious to open a revolving charge account for you. (See page 55)

● That you are buying "balloon bread" without realizing it, fruit drinks that are 90 to 97 per cent water, and pre-sweetened cereals that are 45 per cent sugar (at $1.07 a pound.) (See page 115)

● More than an exposé, *The Innocent Consumer vs. The Exploiters* will give you the protection you need every time you open the door to a salesman. Once you've read this book, you won't be tricked—as so many have—into paying more than $400 for a TV set worth $150 which has false guarantees. And you certainly won't be one of the thousands who have their salaries garnisheed every year without even being notified.
77079

10-Day Free Trial

With all these pitfalls, one sure way to get your money's worth when you buy anything would be to bring along a lawyer, an engineer and a man from the Food and Drug Administration. Much simpler, however, is to go to your bookstore *or* fill out the coupon at right to get your copy of Sidney Margolius' revealing and helpful *The Innocent Consumer vs. The Exploiters.* If you do not believe that this book will save you many times its cost, you may return it within ten days for a full refund.